A
CAMP STORY

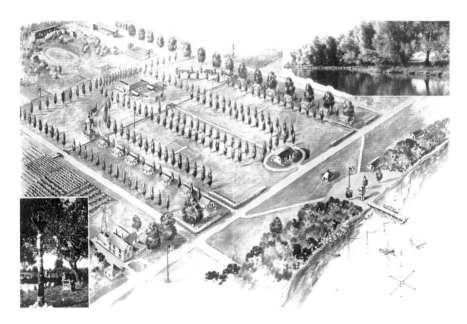

Inaccurate rendering of the camp from the 1941 brochure.

A CAMP STORY

THE HISTORY OF LAKE OF THE WOODS & GREENWOODS CAMPS

DAVID HIMMEL

Charleston · London

THE
History
PRESS

Published by The History Press
Charleston, SC 29403
www.historypress.net

First published 2012

Manufactured in the United States

ISBN 978.1.60949.345.5

Library of Congress CIP data applied for.

"Camp is more than just a summer, more than days spent in play."

—from the song "Camp Is More Than Just a Summer"

For my parents, Jim and Jane.
Thanks for sending me to camp against my will.

CONTENTS

ACKNOWLEDGEMENTS

Every single person I spoke to at any length about this book had a hand in making it possible. But there wouldn't be a book for me to write at all if it weren't for the dear and never-ending friendships of Dan Bates, Doug Bates, James Boulware, Lauren Cohn, Billy Hearth, Liese Hearth, Gerred Howe, Holly Howe, Jeff Miner, Lindsay Saewitz and Rory Zacher.

To the others who supported me in this project and assisted in granting me access to stories, photos and your time, a thank-you: Rob Burns, Dana Cohn, Emily Ferdman, Dan Goldwin, Dayna Hardin, Roselle Hechter, Tod Himmel, Lois Katz, Linda Rosenberg, Agnes Schwartz, Laurie Seeger, Marc Seeger and Sheldon Solow. I couldn't have written word one without Ceil Rothbart. Thank you for the millionth time. Bob Goldwin, thank you for returning my comic books, twenty-two years later.

Thank you to Bill Burghardt and Jordan Burghardt for the incredible creative support and to Joseph Gartrell for doing this with me and keeping me off the ledge. Jarret Keene, thank you for your wisdom and friendship while being both the angel and devil on my hunched writer's shoulders. And thank you to friends and family who may go unnamed here but are never unwritten in my heart.

And of course, to Louis and Florence Greenberg, thank you for taking us camping.

INTRODUCTION

It had been nearly thirty years since Dan Langell worked at Greenwoods Camp. Yet he walked down the beaten path that cut through the sports field toward the cabin area like no time had passed. The wrinkles on his face and the loose skin of age proved otherwise.

Jeff Miner was standing by the Boys' Rec Lodge. The heir apparent to Dan's program director legacy, Miner recognized him immediately.

"Mr. Langell," Miner said, shaking the old man's hand. "It's great to see you. We met years ago, I'm Jeff Miner. I know your son, Dave. We worked together. How are you? What brings you up here?"

"How's camp going?" Dan asked.

"It's going great."

"Good."

"Would you like to take a look around? I'll go get the golf cart."

"No. No, that's all right." He looked past Miner at the ten red cabins horseshoed around the flagpole where the Greenwoods flag hung and watched a couple of campers run into the Boys' Rec Lodge to play basketball. Then he turned around and walked back to the car waiting for him at the road and took off down 47th1/2 Street. Miner watched the car disappear past the baseball field backstop and the Timber Trails sign before going to the Program Cabin to make the announcement for lunch.

Instead of walking with campers or any of his staff members like usual, Miner walked alone and said to himself, "That was…odd." He stopped at the Big House and made a phone call.

"Dave, it's Jeff...Miner. How are you?...Good...Yeah, yeah, I'm great, listen. You're not going to believe this, but I just saw your dad...Yeah, at camp."

It was a surprise to Dave that his father would be anywhere far from home in Indiana and certainly a shock that he was all the way up at camp. His father had dementia. He'd had it for years. His lady friend must've driven him there, he told Miner. Dave and Miner found it curious that Dan would go to camp to just sort of...check in.

Our memories allow us incredible privileges. They allow us to remember the wonderful times and make the horrible not seem so bad. We can relive in reverie at will. Our memories allow us to travel in time at the speed of thought. We don't need a Delorean to take us there. Our memories are the building blocks that make us who we are, and when we lose them, we lose ourselves.

So there's something to be said about a man who, in the grip of madness and without global cognitive ability, was drawn with a great but simple concern to a place where he spent only a few summers of his life. And that something is, "I get it. And that's pretty damn cool."

These pages are made of memories. They're real. These things happened, even if they've changed slightly through the passing of time. This is how the truth is remembered. This is how Lake of the Woods and Greenwoods Camps are remembered. These memories, all these stories, are the memoirs of camp. They're the stories about a place and time unlike any other, where it is safe and a whole lot of fun to grow up.

Not every single story that happened at camp is in this book, and the things you read may not be exactly as you remember them, but that's because you weren't the only person experiencing them. And that right there is what makes all of these stories so special, so different from any other stories we could tell from other parts of our lives. All of our memories of camp are shared. No matter if you were a camper in 1941, a counselor in 1984, a cook in 1990 or a camper in 2011, the memories will be the same. Just change a few names and dates and the story is yours, just as it happened to you. Mostly anyway.

And that's comforting. Because I, for one, hope to God that when I finally lose my mind, when I'm at the thin line of mania and forgetfulness, I've got some nice girl to drive me to the one place I could always remember—camp. Because if I can find my way to the Boys' Program Cabin, then I'm not completely lost. And hopefully, I can tell a camp story. And if so, I'll always know who I am and where I came from.

Chapter I

THE GREENBERG ORPHANS

There is a kind of virtue that lies not in extraordinary actions, not in saving poor orphans from burning buildings, but in steadfastly working for a world where orphans are not poor and buildings comply with decent fire codes.
—Randy Cohen

If you want to completely understand something, you have to know where it came from, why it came to be and who is responsible for what it is. The story of Lake of the Woods and Greenwoods Camps doesn't start with the first summer. It starts with the beginning, with an orphan.

There's a misconception for many that an orphan is little more than a filthy child in fingerless gloves living on a diet of gruel and having no family. And that's nonsense. In this case, the orphan boy we need to talk about was an orphan because he had *too* much family.

Israel Louis Greenberg, who officially went by I. Louis Greenberg and conversationally as Louis, was born in Brooklyn, New York, on September 14, 1890. He was the tenth of thirteen brothers and sisters. That placed him somewhere just outside of being a middle child, sparing him from typical middle child awkwardness.

His father, Solomon Greenberg, was born in Lithuania in about 1833. Daddy was a peddler and married a little later in life, when he was about forty-three. The woman's name was Esther Hannah something-or-other. There is no known record of her actual surname. By the time they were married, Solomon and Esther already had half a dozen children together, and the stage was set for a big, happy, Jewish, Lithuanian home, with all the trappings a family in late nineteenth-century Lithuania would enjoy. But soon after their marriage, Esther died, leaving the peddler and his brood to fend for themselves.

But Solomon was quite the catch, and he quickly fell in love and married again—this time to Betsy Bryna Bertha Pulinsky, who was thirty-five years his junior. And although Solomon came prepackaged with a big family, he and Betsy wanted more—seven more. One of these seven was Louis.

Soon after Solomon and Betsy were married, the family immigrated to the United States and made Brooklyn their home. The thing was that Brooklyn, at the time, was not a safe place for Jews. And according to Solomon's granddaughter, Esther (likely named for her deceased grandmother), it was especially unsafe for Jewish men with beards. And Solomon had a very thick beard, one that was asking for trouble.

On an early summer night on June 18, 1887, Solomon was beaten to death with stones—brutally attacked by Jew- and beard-hating hoodlums. The official cause, according to the death certificate, was "cerebral apoplexy." That means that he was rendered unconscious and died almost as soon as the attack began. Louis was just six years old.

This left Betsy as a single mother. Although the six kids from Solomon's first marriage were grown and out of the house, Betsy had her seven to care for. The oldest, Harry, had just turned fifteen, and the baby, Frances, was only seven months old.

Any money that Solomon may have left for Betsy would have quickly run out. Today, one would think that when a mother of seven becomes a widow, friends and family and other members of the community will step up to offer money and other assistance. But no one was in a place to help then. America was experiencing its greatest depression to date since the economy tanked in the Panic of 1893.

While the 1880s saw a boom of economic expansion due in part to the railroad industry, by 1893 greed had taken over. The railroad expansion became railroad *speculation*, and stability began to waver when railroads were overbuilt. Railroad companies filed for bankruptcy, banks failed and a credit crunch ensued. Farmers in the Midwest were experiencing a terrible drought, making it hard to pay their debts, which drove down land value. Some estimates put unemployment rates as high as 18 percent. It wasn't until 1897 that the economy started to pick up. But as we know well from today's economic situation, rebuilding financial stability does not happen overnight. And there simply was no option to apply for government assistance—no food stamps and no welfare checks. The United

States would not have an organized welfare system for another twenty-six years when President Franklin Roosevelt instituted his New Deal.

Unable to afford all seven children and left with the emotional demands of raising a large family, Betsy was faced with a tough decision. She sent Morris (twelve), Louis (six) and Barney (five) to the Brooklyn Hebrew Orphan Asylum. But giving up your kids wasn't an uncommon practice in the late 1800s. Many asylums took in these half-orphans—children who were part of a family where one of the parents was missing from the picture and the other couldn't afford them. Most often, the missing parent was a father who had run off rather than one viciously murdered like Solomon.

With Harry being fifteen, there was no need to send him away to be looked after. Besides, at that age, he might have been helpful to Betsy and serve as the man of the house. The two girls, Mary and Frances, were too young for Brooklyn Hebrew, which wouldn't take children under the age of four. That left David, who was nine. Why Betsy chose to keep David and hand off the other boys isn't known, but she must have had her reasons. It's a good thing that she sent the younger Louis instead of his older brother. If she hadn't, you wouldn't be reading this book.

The orphanage was more than a boardinghouse. Academic lessons were taught, as were trade skills such as shoemaking and printing for the boys and domestic skills for the girls. On holidays, the children were shuttled off to various neighborhood synagogues.

Louis and Barney did what they could to get by, but Morris was coming apart at the seams. A teenage boy, likely angry with his mother's decision and rebelling against the brass at the orphanage, he cut out and ran away. But Louis stuck it out. In fact, he rather enjoyed it.

When it came time for Louis to leave Brooklyn Hebrew, he stayed and became a caretaker. When he graduated high school and enrolled in Columbia University, he chose child care as his major. And although many college kids want to fly as far from the nest as possible, Louis hung around Brooklyn Hebrew and kept working as a caretaker in exchange for room and board. He was building a reputation for himself. And word got out that he was one of the best caretakers in the system. That's when Chicago came calling.

Chicago and Louis were kindred spirits. Most of Chicago's orphans during the nineteenth century were, in fact, half-orphans like Louis. By the turn of the century, many of those in half-orphan situations still lingered. Orphanages were being attacked by progressive reformers like Jane Addams for being what she considered little more than kiddie warehouses that operated without the children's best intentions in mind. The reformers wanted all half-orphans to be kept at home, with no option of institutional care. Still, through the noise of their shouts, asylums continued to be built throughout the city.

One of these was the Marks Nathan Orphan Home, which was opened in 1906 in the city's Southwest Side. It was named after a wealthy Chicago businessman and was one of the first and few Jewish orphanages in town. A committee from Marks Nathan came to New York to meet with Louis. The committee interviewed him once, and that was the end of it. He was hired, and he immediately packed his bags, left Brooklyn Hebrew and his studies behind and headed off to Chicago.

He was a firm believer in institutional care. The reformers may have had their ideas for what was best for every child in town, but Louis knew better because he had lived it. He was raised in it. And he saw what advantages it could provide for young people. He wanted to take care of children and help them grow in a place where they could feel safe and enjoy their young lives. The Marks Nathan Home allowed him every opportunity, including meeting a young looker named Florence Poncher.

Florence was born in the West Side of Chicago in 1897 to Russian immigrants. She was the fifth oldest out of ten and the youngest of three girls. All of them were chockfull of smarts and wit like their father, Morris. One of her younger brothers, Richard, was a friend of Al Capone after forging a clever business relationship in the 1920s. Richard heard about an armored car company that was going under, and he approached the mobster for a loan to buy the company so that he could build armored cars for Capone and his associates. Richard later became a kind of legend when, in the 1960s, he bought the crypt plot above Marilyn Monroe from her ex-husband and baseball great, Joe DiMaggio, after a chance meeting in a Beverly Hills restaurant. Richard wanted what every heterosexual man in America wanted during the 1950s and '60s: to lay on top of Marilyn Monroe. Since he was already married and Marilyn was already dead, he figured that this was the only surefire way to make that dream come true. And when he died in 1986, he was laid to rest facedown dressed in a fine white suit. The crypt went up for auction on eBay in 2009 but was never sold.

Florence was far more reserved than her brother but had that sharp Poncher mind, and she reveled in her studies. She attended the Jewish Training School of Chicago, which was located near her home in the predominantly

Russian-Jewish neighborhood. She enjoyed that neighborhood and got a real kick out of the school. It was designed to focus on the true development of the students beyond reading, writing and arithmetic. Because so many of the attendees were direct from Russia, the curriculum maintained an aim at teaching English, honing in on the individual's skills and interests and then fostering growth in those specific areas.

Before graduating, however, her family moved south to the thriving Englewood neighborhood. The Ponchers weren't hard for cash, so in what may have been the beginning of appreciating the finer things, she and her older sister, Celia, were driven to school in a limousine.

Florence started volunteering at the Marks Nathan Home when she was fourteen years old. Her father didn't believe that his daughters should have to work, but she was determined to do something other than wait for a husband to come along and live her life for her. With a twinge of irony, this motivation to work would indeed land her in the arms of a man. Although she spent nearly every day at the orphanage, she didn't meet her future husband for another year. When it happened, she and Louis fell in love quickly and completely. They were married a year later in 1914.

Even at that young age, Florence was showing her business smarts and had a strong commitment of service to her community. Two years later, she became involved with what was then known as the Jewish Charities, later renamed the Federated Jewish Charities. She landed a great job as a caseworker where she would go around and interview people in the community to assess living situations and see what could be done to improve people's well-being. What she found was that there was a great need to help the children.

Quickly, Florence gathered her friends, and in 1916, they organized the Jewish Big Sisters. The purpose was for members to be role models and offer mentoring, support and friendship to the girls. The women took them out, provided them with clothes and, more generally, put a little fun in their lives. Florence served as the organization's first president, and throughout her life, she maintained great pride in the work that she and her friends did in the organization's early days, often beaming that she and the ladies must have done well because the organization was still in operation. And more than ninety-five years after its inception, Jewish Big Sisters is still putting fun in girls' lives. Florence might have gone on to do incredible things as the leader of Jewish Big Sisters, but fate had other plans, and she left her position shortly after accepting it.

Louis was tapped to head up a new orphanage in the Great White North. The Jewish Orphanage and Children's Aid of Western Canada was located in Winnipeg, Manitoba. Louis went north to examine the situation, while Florence stayed back waiting for their first child to arrive. Their daughter, Toba, was born on May 17, 1917, and soon enough, both Greenberg girls were in Winnipeg with Louis. Two years later, Florence gave birth to another baby, a boy this time. Seymour Kenneth was born on May 12, 1919, in Chicago. Florence may have loved Winnipeg, but she wanted her children to be American.

The first three years at the orphanage were spent in cramped quarters. The grounds had two small cottages expected to house and educate the children. At first, this was all the room that was needed. But more kids kept coming, and the living conditions quickly became deplorable. The orphanage needed improvements, and Louis told the board of directors just that. The board supported his zeal, but he would have to raise the money. Like his wife had done with the needy girls in Chicago, he sprung into high-octane action mode. Louis went on a tear, raising capital for the orphanage. He toured much of western Canada, where he gave speeches and collected money. And in just a few months, he, along with the help of some of his friends, had raised nearly $100,000. In today's dollars, that's almost $1.9 million.

With the cash in place, it was easy to build a more appropriate home for the orphanage. And in 1920, a three-and-a-half-story building was erected on five acres, complete with a playground, a skating rink and a large, two-acre garden. This is where the Jewish Orphanage and Children's Aid of Western Canada remained until it was closed in 1947. The building was demolished in 1962. A dedicated park of oak trees is there instead.

Happy with the accommodations that he had brought about, Louis and Florence were able to give the children the life they thought all children deserved—an enjoyable one. There were 150 children living at the orphanage at any one time. The kids attended public school but were also dosed with daily lessons in Hebrew and Jewish traditions. Daily religious services and a children's choir rounded out the Jewish experience.

The friendship they received from the people in Winnipeg was unbelievable. Years later, Florence called it "wonderful kindness." It gave them a feeling of warmth and understanding, and they were able to give that back to the children, whom Louis and Florence loved as their own.

All was running smoothly at the home, and the Greenbergs were hard-pressed to find anything to complain about. Then, a little more than a year after Seymour was born, there was a breakout of scarlet fever. Irritating rashes, painful sore throats, delusional high fevers and sinus infections riddled the home. Louis, Florence and the staff did what they could to fend off the disease and keep the children as comfortable as possible, but the thing about scarlet fever is that it likes young children. And in a home of 150 to choose from, it was like a complimentary Las Vegas buffet for the disease. Things became harder after Florence contracted the disease herself and was rendered out of commission when she was sent to the hospital with the others. Louis was frantic with concern and worry. On top of that, his toddler son also got sick.

Today, if you catch a case of scarlet fever, you take some antibiotics and you're back in business in twenty-four hours. But this was late 1920. George Fredrick Dick and his wife, Gladys Henry Dick, wouldn't develop their scarlet fever vaccine for another three years. As it was, Seymour Greenberg died due to complications from scarlet fever on May 29, 1920.

A parent losing a child is an unnatural experience. It messes with the natural order of things. All their lives, Louis and Florence sought to give children a better and great life. It didn't matter where the kids came from or how they got there. If a kid showed up at the door, the Greenbergs were there to lend not just a hand but an entire appendage. But they couldn't protect everyone all of the time—even their baby boy.

Those years in Winnipeg were good ones. Both Louis and Florence were happy with the work they did, and the children and families involved with the Jewish Orphanage and Children's Aid of Western Canada still regarded Louis with reverence decades later. But when Seymour died, the appeal of Winnipeg died, too. Soon, Louis, Florence and Toba moved stateside to Chicago's Rogers Park.

In an interview at the Winnipeg Jewish Community Council office on July 13, 1981, Florence said, "I love Winnipeg. I so often thought, 'Oh, if only we hadn't left, maybe life would have been different for us.'"

Chapter 2

FINDING DECATUR

The Promised Land always lies on the other side of a wilderness.
—Havelock Ellis

Chicago had a lot going on in the early 1920s. Prohibition was in full swing, which made crime the garnish of choice. There were a reported one thousand gangs claiming various turf throughout the city. Capone was getting his foothold in things corrupt and powerful—perhaps with help from his friend Richard Poncher in the armored car business. Industry was booming and creating hundreds of thousands of jobs. The availability of work attracted just as many black people from the southern states in what was later called the Great Migration. Other than the work ethic, and hearts full of hope for better lives, these southerners brought with them a musical movement that made Chicago a center for jazz and the lifestyle that accompanied the sound.

Oh yes, make no mistake, these were the Roaring Twenties, complete with speakeasies, mob wars, jazz clubs and flappers. But while Chicago was roaring away, enjoying its fame as a major cultural and business hub, things were a little quieter in the Greenberg house. After returning from Winnipeg a little worse for the wear following Seymour's death, Louis didn't take a job at his old orphanage as one might think. Nor did he find work at a new home. Instead, completely out of character, he stepped into a new and thriving industry.

Florence began writing her life story in a wide-ruled spiral notebook in the 1980s, and in it she wrote, "My father took Louis into his machinery

The Greenberg family. *Left to right*:
Toba, Florence, Deborah and Louis.
Courtesy of Ceil Rothbart.

business, which he was not happy with." Meanwhile, she gave birth to their daughter Deborah on November 17, 1921.

It wasn't long before Louis left the machinery business. But provisions for his young family remained, and he took a job selling insurance. He didn't love this job either, but it was a means to an end. Over the next several years, unbeknownst to anyone else, he started quietly shopping for real estate. Not to invest in or necessarily to build a home on, but rather to use it to build a summer camp for Jewish children. All existing summer camps were restricted, and the market was prime.

It's uncertain why Louis never went back to the orphanage business and opted to build a camp instead. I can only assume that orphanages reminded him of losing Seymour. Maybe he wanted to put every inch of that memory behind him. Maybe he liked the idea of having a place away from the city, out there in the woods among the quiet with the trees, a safe distance from the industry and machines and jazz clubs and drive-bys of Chicago. Maybe he just saw a new opportunity for kids. When a man spends his entire life taking care of children and giving them a place to be happy, he doesn't just turn his back on them in exchange for slinging insurance policies.

The Point of Lake of the Woods, circa 1935. *Courtesy of Lake of the Woods and Greenwoods Camps.*

He found a piece of land in a small, southwestern Michigan farming town called Decatur. The farm sat on fifty-three acres along the west shore of the muddy-bottomed but beautiful Lake of the Woods. It was an ironic find because the orphanage home in Winnipeg was a mere 150 miles northwest of another Lake of the Woods. Perhaps Louis found some comfort in that irony.

The farm had spent the last several decades in a sort of restlessness. It belonged to Milo and Mary Youells, who first saw it as an attraction for summertime fun. The Youellses built a dance hall on the far west end of the property in the hopes of attracting summer boarders. They saw some success, but Mary's health began to fail, and the upkeep and management became too much, so they sold it off to the Decatur Grange. A few years later, the dance hall became the site of Decatur's First Reformed Church.

Then, according to Decatur records, a woman referenced only as Mrs. Gothe bought the farm. She built another dance hall and two cottages. Her plan was to make the farm a full-blown summer resort. But in 1929, shortly after her purchase, the Great Depression hit. In a flash, summer travel and dancing were not a priority for too many midwesterners, and Mrs. Gothe was forced to sell her land. The Kakis family quickly scooped it up and turned it right around to August Tange of Chicago, who remained the owner until Louis purchased it.

Louis found the land for sale through the real estate dealer, William Meulleider of Hartford. Like any responsible parents, Louis and Florence

The farmhouse as it was when Louis purchased it from August Tange in 1935. *Courtesy of Lake of the Woods and Greenwoods Camps.*

put money aside for their children's future. Specifically, mom and dad had stuffed away a fair amount of cash for Toba's college education. But when the future becomes the present and a lot of money is needed quickly, you have to break the piggybank. Louis used Toba's college money to help buy the old farm. As a result, Toba never went to college. But she did go to camp. Really, she helped *build* the camp. In addition to his daughter's money for school, he found an agreeable builder who financed the rest of the project, and soon enough, the Greenbergs were the owners of a summer camp and a mortgage.

Building the camp began immediately in the spring of 1935—not just erecting cabins but also enrolling children to fill them. "There was work started," Florence wrote in her journal. "[We] worked very hard—my parents, brothers, sisters, and others—as my two girls grew up—everyone helped. And we had a happy base group of people."

The Poncher and Greenberg families planted trees, bushes and lilacs. For the next several years, Toba and Deborah's jobs were to hang off the back of their mother's car and water those trees and bushes with watering cans while she drove around the property. Drive-by watering…what family friend Al Capone could have done if he went into botany.

The first incarnation of Lake of the Woods Camp was anything but rustic. There were twenty-two buildings, sixteen of them having been designed to

Seven of the original sixteen cottages, circa 1935. *Courtesy of Lake of the Woods and Greenwoods Camps.*

hold seven campers and one counselor. They were sixteen by twenty-four feet, fitting eight beds, four dressers, a toilet, a sink, a radio and electric lights. Eight of the cottages were described in an article in the *Decatur Republican* as having "sun bathing pavilions with bath tubs for weekly scrubbing." There was the potential for a lot of bathing.

The dance hall turned church, which was twenty-eight by sixty feet, was lifted and moved seven hundred feet west and converted into the first Mess Hall, which held forty tables seating four chairs at each. An additional building measuring twenty square feet was built to serve as a fully functioning electric kitchen, complete with stoves and refrigeration. In 1935, most urban homes and buildings had electricity, but the rural locations were often without. That the camp was going to have an electric kitchen and electric lights in the cottages, as well as many other electric lights throughout the grounds—including several searchlights—is a testament to the length the Greenbergs would go to provide the best conditions for their campers. Even the camp's five original wells were pumped by two electric motors. Edison would have been proud.

In order for all of this electricity to happen, the Michigan Gas and Electric Company extended the lines from highway M-40 near another property known as the Iodent farm a few miles away. This cost the Greenbergs $1,000, which equals a little more than $16,000 today. The entire electric bill for the season in 1935 dollars would be between $600 and $800.

An infirmary was built, with ten beds and all of the necessary equipment. The lakefront was lined with large trees, and among them, two clubhouses were built, one for the boys and the other for the girls. They were filled with easy chairs, books and radios. A watchtower was built for lifeguard supervision. A 105-foot-long pier was put into the lake, and 150 loads of gravel were poured in to solidify the bottom and reduce the lake's muddy sinkholes. This created a safer swimming and recreation area. Four concrete septic tanks were installed, each measuring 4 by 4 by 10 feet, with 6,600 feet of soil pipe and 3,500 feet of water pipe. The ten-room farmhouse situated just off 47th½ Street was remodeled. It became Louis and Florence's summer home, as well as a place for parents to stay when visiting their children. The biggest building on the property, it was cleverly named the Big House. There were about a dozen rented horses for riding activities, four rowboats, six kayaks and two motorboats.

In just a few months, an entire camp was designed and built. Now it was just a matter of filling it up with people. In addition to Louis and Florence, thirty-five staff members worked that first season, twenty-five of them being counselors. All twenty-five were college students from Illinois, Wisconsin or Michigan. A full-time doctor and nurse from Michael Reese Hospital were hired.

This is the first incarnation of the Lake of the Woods Camp waterfront with a lookout tower. *Courtesy of Lake of the Woods and Greenwoods Camps.*

The original Infirmary. It was large enough for ten beds and had a full-time doctor and nurse on staff during the inaugural summer. *Courtesy of Lake of the Woods and Greenwoods Camps.*

The staff was scheduled to arrive at camp in mid-June, about two weeks before opening day. Because no camp program had ever been executed, the staff was tasked with developing the summer's events from scratch. However, there were plans made with the Cozy Theatre in town, located on Phelps Street, for the campers to take in a movie twice a week. The counselors would have to fill in the rest of the time.

That first season's attendance was 125 rambunctious, suburban kids, boys and girls between the ages of six and sixteen. There was only one session. It was nine weeks long. It cost $200 for the whole summer. Lake of the Woods Camp for Boys and Girls was opened on June 29, 1935.

Chapter 3
THE PIONEERS

There is no such word as "can't."

—*early camp motto*

Consider that first day: the smell of fresh paint, saplings lining the roads, the Mess Hall without a crumb on the floor, cabin dressers without a single name carved into them. As the campers arrived, there was no unpacking and then walking around the grounds to look at familiar places. Every step was exploration.

The 1935 campers and counselors had a lot of responsibility to carry. Being first is never easy. Everything you do can set the standard for everything else to come. At the same time, however, it can be exciting to navigate destiny without a map.

Louis had his camp, and finally, after years of suffering through wretched jobs, he was back where he belonged: among kids, providing a safe and encouraging environment for them. Although these kids weren't orphans, some of them were children of the orphans he and Florence had once taken care of. Filling a summer camp with campers has always been a challenge. But Lake of the Woods had a built-in audience. Beyond advertising to Jewish families and friends in Chicago, many families who knew the Greenbergs from Winnipeg sent their children down to Decatur. And although this new family venture was a business, Louis and Florence were more concerned with having kids at camp than the money. In some cases, tuition was waived for the families who couldn't afford it. Once the bills were paid, every other dollar was simply found money.

Louis and Florence Greenberg in front of the Big House in about 1939. *Courtesy of Ceil Rothbart.*

Those first few years, the Great Depression was still raging, and much of America was having a hard time keeping food on the table, but sending their kids to camp was important, and Louis and Florence understood that. Lake of the Woods wasn't there just so kids could ride horses or paddle canoes for a few summer weeks, it was there as an escape from the harsh realities of the modern world. Kids needn't worry about where the next meal was coming from. The Mess Hall provisions were always ample.

In what might be considered record growth, Lake of the Woods got so big so fast that it had to open an entirely new camp. This camp was built on the east side of 47th½ Street. There were five cabins erected and named after states of the Union. The Greenbergs attached their name to this one,

The boys were moved from Lake of the Woods to their own camp in 1937. Welcome to Camp Greenwoods. *Courtesy of Lake of the Woods and Greenwoods Camps.*

and in 1937, just two years after their first summer as camp owners, Camp Greenwoods for Boys was opened. Florence wrote in her personal journal that those days were "wonderful and we thrived."

With the family name adorning the signs, brochures and letterhead, camping was officially a family business. The Lake of the Woods and Greenwoods grounds were teeming with Greenberg and Poncher kinfolk. Toba, now in her mid-twenties, married one of the best things to happen to the camp. Walter Neumann was a mensch by all accounts. In a personal letter from Louis on Greenwoods stationery to his daughter a few years before the marriage, he offered his overwhelming approval of Walter, as well as his unsought blessing for Toba to marry him. He told her that it was more important to have a husband who would care for her than one who would plainly provide. He went as far to say that she wouldn't have to worry about money because the camp was a family affair and was doing quite well financially; he added that she should encourage Walter to join the family business. And unofficially, he did. He kind of had to.

In May 1941, just a month shy of the opening day of the seventh season, Louis Greenberg died. He was fifty-one years old. According to surviving family members, it was kidney failure. He was never hospitalized or treated for any disease. His death came suddenly. His death came tragically. His death came with a widow. For the first time since she was a teenager, Florence was without Louis. She had two camps, a mortgage, a staff and hundreds of children for whom to provide a summer's worth of memories and personal growth. With little to no warning, Florence was now the sole owner and director of Lake of the Woods and Greenwoods Camps. And if the new responsibility put any chink in her armor, you'd never know it. "Camp was Louis' dream," said family historian Ceil Rothbart, Toba and Walter's youngest daughter, "but it became Florence's passion."

So, camp went on. More kids came each year from Chicago and Canada. In fact, there was a very large Canadian contingency at camp for years because of the Winnipeg connection. Many of Florence's siblings sent their kids to camp, making lots of the campers first and second cousins to one another. And like it had been a safe haven away from the rigors of the Great Depression, so was the case when America entered World War II. For the kids and staff at Lake of the Woods and Greenwoods, the war might as well have been in another universe. And with so many parents pitching in with the war effort, it made sense to send the kids away to camp, where mom and dad knew that they'd be looked after and enjoy their time as a kid rather than worry about rubber drives and war bonds.

One of the most exciting offerings of this particular camp was that there was an actual stable with horses on the property. There weren't many boys' camps that offered riding as an activity, and it was even less common that the horses lived at camp throughout the summer. Other camps would take field trips to nearby stables or farms. Florence employed George Bender as the riding instructor. According to campers there at the time, he was a hunk. The girls just loved him. Florence also had the talent of her son-in-law, Walter, who made trips to camp from Chicago on weekends to help out. He was quite good with the horses and, really, with just about anything Florence needed.

Walter worked long days in the stables, handled maintenance issues, rode the tractor to cut the grass before each season opened, made runs into town and truly helped keep the camp moving. On his drives from Chicago, he shuttled rations, and on one particular trip, he ran into trouble with the law. President Eisenhower hadn't yet commissioned the interstate concrete

Left to right: Little Loie Neumann; her father, Walter; and her brother, Kenny, in front of the camp's station wagon. *Courtesy of Ceil Rothbart.*

Mrs. G. at work in the Big House office. She always used green ink pens. That PA system on her desk was wired throughout the camp by her brother, Cookie's dad. *Courtesy of Ceil Rothbart.*

arteries, and the roads between Chicago and Decatur made for a long ride. Florence preferred to get certain foods from a family member back in the city because she could make purchases at wholesale prices. And in a hurry to get up to camp with a trunk full of bananas, Walter was pulled over for speeding by a local cop, somewhere in Indiana. Capitalizing on guilt as an ally, Walter talked his way out of the ticket by exclaiming, "I've got a trunk full of bananas! You don't want these children to starve, do you?"

Walter worked hard, and he was good to have around. Florence was a hard worker, too, but preferred to stay clean and handle the administrative side of the business. She needed to be at camp with the kids and didn't have time to talk her way out of speeding tickets. Plus, she only drove on camp property. Not obsessive over money, Florence did enjoy life's niceties. Throughout the summer, no matter how hot, she always wore dresses or handmade gabardine trousers. And she drove her woodie station wagon to the Mess Hall from the Big House. She could have easily been perceived as the queen of the camp, ruling over her kingdom of campers and counselors from her white farmhouse castle and traveling in regal style. But that characterization would be wrong. She was approachable and loved by everyone who met her—kids, parents, staff, everyone. To them, she was just Mrs. G.

Getting up to Mrs. G.'s camp was the start of the adventure. To avoid the long haul of the roads, and Indiana cops, parents tossed their kids on the Illinois Central Railroad. Four cars were blocked off specifically for the campers. This kept the childish rowdiness from mixing with the general, paying public. The majority of Chicagoans attending camp were southsiders. And when the train made a stop in Park Forest, some kids climbed out of the train car windows in an attempt to head back home. But these kids were newbies and didn't know what joys awaited them in Decatur.

Agnes Gabanyi had only been in the United States for six months when she showed up at Lake of the Woods. She was thirteen years old. After two years of living in war-ravaged Europe, Agnes and her father came to the United States as the only two family members who survived the Holocaust. Right away he was diagnosed with tuberculosis and shipped off to the Chicago-Winfield Tuberculosis Sanitarium, where Central DuPage Hospital now stands. He was there almost a year before being declared a negative case. But he had trouble assimilating to American culture and couldn't learn the language, so he went back to Hungary, leaving Agnes in the care of her mother's sister's family.

The young girl had no idea what to expect from camp. "My cousins had been there before," Agnes said. "I had no expectations, good or bad. I was a stranger in unfamiliar territory."

As if being a thirteen-year-old girl wasn't hard enough, she barely knew a lick of English, she had no friends and the family she grew up with and loved was gone. Thirteen years in, she was starting from scratch. She was a klutz, too. But she found comfort in the water, where she was a white cap swimmer, the highest level a camper could obtain. In descending order, there were white cap, blue cap, yellow cap and red cap swim levels. It wasn't long before she made friends, lots of good friends. "These friends lifted me out of my loneliness at a difficult time of my life," she said. "At camp, we were a family—lots of cheers but never any jeers." And Agnes received a lot of those cheers when she exercised her newfound skill and swam across the lake. "I felt ten feet tall."

By the end of the summer, Agnes had improved her English and become Americanized, as she puts it. She also learned about bras.

On her sixteenth birthday in July, her cabin mates surprised her with a gift: a navy blue, long-sleeved cashmere sweater. Cashmere is nice material, and for Agnes, it might as well have been material weaved by the holy angels

Lake of the Woods white cap swimmers. *Courtesy of Lake of the Woods and Greenwoods Camps.*

themselves. "That sweater was so dear to me that after I wore a hole in the elbow, I cut the sleeves short and hemmed them so I could continue wearing it as a short-sleeved sweater."

No camp was ever designed to be a formal place. But Lake of the Woods and Greenwoods had its more formal moments. Regardless of the heat, Friday night Shabbat services required the campers to don their finest of wears. Girls wore their cashmere sweaters and gabardine slacks, and boys tucked in buttoned-down shirts with nice slacks. On Sundays, the girls wore their whites: shorts and blouses with Lake of the Woods embroidered on the pocket. Uniforms were required every day—suggested, really. They consisted of brown socks and brown shorts, with a Lake of the Woods or Greenwoods shirt. Only the new or younger campers wore the uniforms daily. Seasoned vets brought their own styles. Levi's jeans were a must.

The girls played a lot of jacks in the cabin. Close friends Alice Andrews Schindel, Beverly Cooper, Cookie Poncher Medansky and Marilyn

Playing jacks on the stoop of Louis Lodge. *Courtesy of Lake of the Woods and Greenwoods Camps.*

Camp Greenwoods picture day. *Courtesy of Lake of the Woods and Greenwoods Camps.*

Lieberman Liberman spent time at what they called the Dream Tree. As campers, when everything seems bigger to the tiny child's eye, they thought that they were venturing out far into the expanse of what is today's golf range. But it was the big oak tree just behind the girls' recreation lodge, called Louis Lodge, near the old silo base. "Four of us would go there," said Cookie. "The leaves came down low, all the way to the ground. It was like a hut. And we'd lie down and nap and talk about girl things. Like boys and shaving our legs and bras and who supposedly kissed who."

Cookie was one of those many family members who made camp their summertime home. Mrs. G. was her aunt. Cookie first came to camp when she was five years old and stayed in the Big House with her Aunt Florence and Florence's mother, who would often go to camp to be with her widowed daughter. Cookie was terrified when she witnessed Grandma taking her teeth out at the end of the day and hanging her sheitel, the wig worn by married orthodox Jewish women, on the back of her bedroom door and brushing it. "I didn't want to go back there. Ever," Cookie said.

But she did go back, of course, as did so many others. They went back for the friends they were making, the adventures they were having, the songs they were writing and the traditions they were starting. Many of them took place around the campfire, like Honor Camper. Each Sunday, the camp would gather at the Girls' Campfire by the lake. They sang and shared stories, and as the smoke danced up and into the stars, a far-off counselor dressed as an Indian called out the week's Honor Campers' names. They were those campers who displayed kindness, friendship and good camp spirit. The qualifications are the genesis of the Seven Virtues, which were the frame for the summer's Color Days. Each Honor Camper received a small plaque and a torch while the "Honor Camper Song" was sung. Back at the cabins, once everyone was tucked in, the counselors stood outside the cabins and continued to serenade the girls. At the end of the summer, the Honor Campers were celebrated again in a large ceremony. It was something each Lake of the Woods camper looked forward to being named. Well, each camper except Lois Neumann, Toba and Walter's daughter (Mrs. G.'s granddaughter).

"I promise to live up to the standards set for the worthy position of Honor Camper. I will be loyal, true, sincere, friendly and always carry a warm fire in my heart for my fellow campers. I will work hand in hand with my counselors and associates and do all in my power to lighten their burden. If I fail in my promise, may I be disqualified as an Honor Camper."

—Honor Camper Pledge

"I was never a goody-two-shoes," Lois said laughing. "I was too much of a rebel, I suppose. Even nepotism wouldn't work for me." It's not that she was a bad kid or not well liked; it's just that she preferred mischief. Lois would short-sheet beds, put plastic wrap over the toilets, take the springs off the beds and turn the dresser drawers upside down so when they were opened, all the contents would dump out onto the floor. Mostly, she pranked her counselors. Known as Little Loie, Lois Neumann Katz spent her first years at camp in a crib in the Big House and moved into a cabin when she was only three years old in 1946.

The History of Lake of the Woods and Greenwoods Camps

"I had Lois as a camper for several years," said Roselle Redman Hechter, a camper and counselor from 1941 to 1954, as well as Lois's favorite counselor. "She would tell people that if anything went wrong, she was going to tell Nony about it. She may have been difficult at times, but I always made sure she toed the line…She would wander into the Big House, and Mrs. G. would offer her candy. But she'd say, 'Oh no, I can't take any unless I have enough for everybody. My counselor said.'"

Roselle enjoyed every advantage of camp. She was a great horseback rider and became an Honor Camper, a Color Days captain and, eventually, the waterfront director. Plus, she met her husband, Raymond, while working at camp.

There were other favorite new traditions, like the Wishing Boat Ceremony at the end of the summer. Each camper had his or her own mock sailboat, a small piece of wood with a point in front and a hole for a candle in back. They would write special wishes on the sails and then feed them through the wooden dowels, light the candles and send them out into the lake. "Our wishes would be something like, 'I hope I can come back next summer,' or something about boys," Lois said. "We were doing wonderful things for the environment, I'll tell you," she said laughing. "Those boats are probably all at the bottom of the lake alongside the diamond ring I lost."

There was an impenetrable safety at camp, even throughout the polio epidemic of the late 1940s and early '50s. Polio is a virus that can affect the central nervous system, causing paralysis and/or death. It's surprising that it wasn't a bigger concern at camp because of the way it can quickly spread and because of its increased prevalence during summer and autumn months. It's a filthy disease. Polio is spread primarily through the fecal-oral route. Simply put, if water is contaminated with fecal matter and it gets in your mouth, like say when you're splashing around in a lake, you could get sick. In 1949, 2,720 polio-related deaths were reported in the United States. By 1952, the country experienced the worst outbreak when 3,145 people died. Nearly 2,000 of the dead were children. In 1955, Dr. Jonas Salk discovered the polio vaccine, making it a disease not to be feared. Well, other than the fear of having crapwater in your mouth.

But there never was a polio outbreak at Lake of the Woods or Greenwoods. In fact, Alice was sent to camp to get away from the polio in Chicago the summer of 1948. Toba, however, was concerned about the disease. Among the family, she was the only one. Though her husband; their eldest, Kenny; and Lois took fondly to camp life, Toba preferred hotel beds to bunk cots, as did her youngest, Ceil. On top of the polio phobia, Toba was concerned that her mother was getting too old for camp and that her husband was working too hard. Walter not only helped out during the summer, but because Mrs. G. didn't drive in the city, he also drove her to prospective campers' families all winter long to talk to them about the camp. He was a damn good son-in-law, that Walter.

By the early 1950s, Mrs. G. was feeling pressure from Toba to sell the camp and move on to the next stage in her life. But things were going well, and she still had work to do. In 1952, Lake of the Woods got a face-lift when ten new brick cabins were built parallel to $47^{th}\frac{1}{2}$ Street, under the shade of trees and with a shower in each one. Instead of being named with numbers, they were named after women's colleges, like Vassar, Sarah Lawrence and Bryn Mawr. Most of the original cottages were torn down, taking with them walls adorned in graffiti made up of the names of all the girls who lived in them over the previous seventeen years. Only a handful of original cabins remained on the south side of the road. One of these was

The new Lake of the Woods cabins, 1952. *Courtesy of Lake of the Woods and Greenwoods Camps.*

moved and attached to the side of the Big House closest to Louis Lodge. It was converted into a storage garage for Canteen items. Those walls were never painted over, and the names and dates remained. The camp was growing, and the new cabins were bigger, with higher ceilings so they could accommodate more kids and bunk beds if needed. These new brick cabins were very modern and remain so today.

It took some time, but eventually, Mrs. G. decided to leave camp. Years later, Ceil asked her grandmother why she sold the camp. Her answer? "Your mother convinced me." It was Louis' plan to have Lake of the Woods and Greenwoods stay in the family, but there was no one old enough or willing enough to take the reins from Mrs. G. It may not have been a Greenberg who would own the camp next, but it would become a multigenerational family affair. And when Mrs. G. left Decatur behind, she left behind a camp with an incredible reputation and one that had an undeniable effect on the lives of thousands of campers and counselors.

Rather than sit around twiddling her thumbs in retirement, Walter convinced her to do some traveling. So, Florence struck out to see the world, with Decatur now a pin in her map of memories.

Chapter 4

SEEGERVILLE

How pleasant it is for a father to sit at his child's board. It is like an aged
man reclining under the shadow of an oak, which he has planted.
—Voltaire

Mrs. G. didn't have to look far to find a buyer. For years, the place to buy any and all things summer camp in Chicago was either Marshall Field's or Mandel Brothers department stores. Both had summer camp departments at which the experts recommended camps to interested shoppers, with various camp brochures at the ready. This was where camp families could buy camp gear like logoed shirts and shorts, among other things.

Lawrence "Laurie" Seeger, a lifelong Boy Scout and camping fanatic, had his ears and eyes peeled for a camp to purchase. One day in 1955, he made his usual reconnaissance stop at Mandel Brothers, where Jennie Purvin, a leader in the Jewish women's progressive movement, let him know that Florence Greenberg was looking to sell her camp in Decatur, Michigan. Laurie's lifelong goal was about to be realized: "I was one of the few people who knew what I wanted to do. I wanted to be a camp director."

From age twelve, Laurie had been hooked on camping. He spent his childhood in the woods with the Boy Scouts and became the youngest director of the Owasippe Scout Reservation camp in Twin Lake, Michigan. At the end of his senior prom, his date drove him directly to the train station, where he was Los Angeles bound to work at Camp Max Strauss, a new camp designed to serve underprivileged children. It was a program started by the Jewish Big Brothers and Big Sisters of Los Angeles. He was going to college, and in April 1943, when he was just three courses short of graduating, the United States government came looking for him. They needed more men for the war. So, Laurie went off to serve in the U.S. Army Air Corps.

When he returned to Chicago, he became active in the Young Men's Jewish Council of Chicago, the Boys Club and the Boys Brotherhood Republic. He married Phyllis Renberg, and they had two sons, Marc and Jerry. He taught elementary fiscal education and was a guidance counselor. His commitment to working with kids was rewarding, but Laurie was a camper by nature, and school classrooms are not ideal places for building campfires. He worked hard to provide for his family while hunting the dream of owning a camp.

So when Jennie gave him the news, he acted quickly. He procured a loan for $10,000 with business partner Chris Vee. This partnership allowed a bounty for Laurie because several years after Lake of the Woods and Greenwoods were bought, two other brother-sister camps were purchased. These were in Green Lake, Wisconsin, and called Sandstone Camp for Girls and Day-Cho-Lah Camp for Boys. Laurie ran the camps in Decatur, while Chris handled the ones in Green Lake. Both Sandstone and Day-Cho-Lah were closed in 1972 after nearly sixty years in operation.

In 1956, Laurie's first summer as owner and director of Lake of the Woods and Greenwoods Camps, there were ninety girls and sixty boys. It was more of a transitional year than anything. Mrs. G. was still around to help out with administrative issues and to make the transition seamless. Still, Laurie began making changes immediately.

There weren't any pine trees on the property, so Laurie planted pines throughout. The boys' cabin names were changed from states to Native American tribes. There were even pictures of the various Indian chiefs put up in the cabins. He was able to have the telephone company give a telephone pole to the camp so a totem pole could be made. Chuck Cooper, the arts instructor, oversaw the project while boys carved it out near the Boys' Rec Lodge. It took two years to complete, and finally, in 1958, the Lake of the Woods and Greenwoods totem pole was erected near the Boys' Campfire Circle in front of the Big House. It stayed there until 1971. Laurie wanted patriotism at camp, too. Many of the American flags that flew over the two camps once flew over the United States Capitol. Laurie requested them from United States senators like Edward McKinley Dirksen of Illinois.

The Boys' Rec Lodge, originally called Florence Lodge, was renamed Thunderbird Lodge. Louis Lodge was dropped and was simply called the Girls' Rec Lodge. The horseback-riding ring, which was originally in the

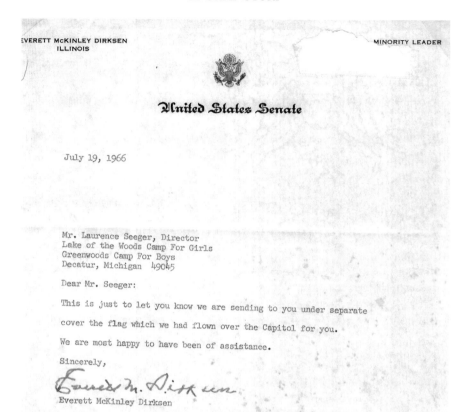

EVERETT McKINLEY DIRKSEN
ILLINOIS

MINORITY LEADER

United States Senate

July 19, 1966

Mr. Laurence Seeger, Director
Lake of the Woods Camp For Girls
Greenwoods Camp For Boys
Decatur, Michigan 49045

Dear Mr. Seeger:

This is just to let you know we are sending to you under separate
cover the flag which we had flown over the Capitol for you.

We are most happy to have been of assistance.

Sincerely,

Everett McKinley Dirksen

Laurie Seeger encouraged pride in one's country. Many flags that were run up the flagpoles once flew over the United States Capitol Building. This is one letter noting the coming authentic flag. *Courtesy of Lake of the Woods and Greenwoods Camps.*

field behind the Big House, now the golf range, was moved across the street and attached to the stables. Laurie named the ring Twinwoods Corral. A teepee was set up near the barn and was lit each night with Japanese lanterns. A covered wagon was placed nearby. A large sign was hung in an open area between the lake and the riding ring that read "Campcraft." This was the designated area where kids learned their outdoor skills. He found and converted old buggy wheels into lamps. They were hung in all of the boys' cabins and throughout the Mess Hall. The new, rustic chandeliers in the Mess Hall were outfitted with flame-shaped light bulbs. "I wanted to give the place a certain look," Laurie said. "I wanted to make it more campy." When he aimed for "campy," he didn't mean campy in the ridiculous sense but rather more rustic and Native American–like. More like the Boy Scout camps he was used to.

The History of Lake of the Woods and Greenwoods Camps

The Twinwoods Ranch and Riding Corral. Laurie moved the horseback riding classes from across the road to be connected to the stables. The old riding ring was turned into a golf driving range and a small course. *Courtesy of Lake of the Woods and Greenwoods Camps.*

Lake of the Woods girls learning outdoor living skills in the early 1960s. *Courtesy of Lake of the Woods and Greenwoods Camps.*

Aerial view of the entire camp waterfront, circa 1968. *Courtesy of Lake of the Woods and Greenwoods Camps.*

Order of the Arrowhead Indians prepare for the ceremony. *Courtesy of Lake of the Woods and Greenwoods Camps.*

He expanded water skiing and purchased Sunfish sailboats, as well as one larger sailboat for group instruction named the *Sunbird*. With the upgrades to the waterfront, he maintained the Greenberg-era practice of having sand and gravel dumped onto the ice covering the lake in the winter so the mud bottom would be safer for swimming.

Sticking with the campy/Native American theme, ceremonies like Indian Princess and Order of the Arrowhead were instituted. These new programs replaced Honor Camper but still recognized campers who displayed the best citizenship or kindness or camp spirit. Originally, like Honor Camper, Indian Princesses and Arrowheads were elected by their peers. But instead of the ceremony happening once a week, it occurred once per session, every four weeks. The pomp and circumstance was far more ritualistic, like Indian ceremonies with costumes, war paint and drums.

> *"My friends, it has been agreed that in the third and seventh weeks of the camp season, a selection shall be made by the campers of those who are the best campers at Greenwoods Camp. It is a great honor to be selected."*
>
> *—Order of the Arrowhead Ceremony*
>
> *"You have been chosen to become a member of the Lake of the Woods Society. This is an honor, but not an easy honor. If you decide to accept the offer of membership in the Society, there will be ahead of you a time of hardship and trial. I can tell you no more."*
>
> *—Indian Princess Ceremony*

The inductees slept outdoors and were only permitted to speak to counselors, former Indian Princesses or Arrowheads and one another. It was like a less violent version of Fight Club but with more headdresses.

> *"I had that mosquito that wouldn't leave my ear that night. And we slept right next to the stables. Whose idea was that?"*
>
> *—Dan Goldwin, camper/counselor 1981–90*

The next day, they were tasked with what can only be considered manual labor. All around camp that day, inductees wore new Indian-themed necklaces, picked up trash, mended fences and did other duties. But it was an honor that most kids wanted. It made you a part of something that anyone could earn. But you had to earn it. And once earned, it was yours.

For all of the changes Laurie was making, they were only aesthetic. The spirit of camp did not change at all. There was even familiarity in the way family played a big part in keeping the programs and the day-to-day events going. Laurie came to camp with Phyllis, Marc and Jerry.

The boys were too young to help out, so they enjoyed being campers, although Marc, only six years old that first summer, was terribly homesick, even with his parents just across the road in the Big House. Phyllis began writing the camp manual. Mrs. G. left behind some program guidebooks, but there was not much in the way of how to take a trip outside camp. As Jerry got older, he helped write many of the activity manuals. Unlike her

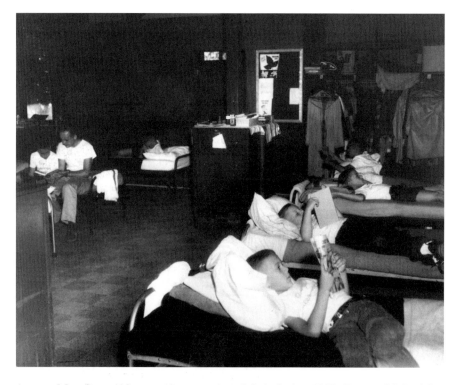

A young Marc Seeger (closest to the camera) reads in bed, circa 1961. *Courtesy of Lake of the Woods and Greenwoods Camps.*

husband, Phyllis wasn't one to live and breathe camp. After a number of summers in Decatur, she stayed home while the men went camping.

If the Seegers were Lake of the Woods' and Greenwoods' first family, the Langells were a close second. Dan Langell was a high school principal in Indianapolis. He was hired in 1960 as the boys' program director. His wife, Lorraine, was hired, too. She spent her first few summers as the waterfront director before becoming the girls' program director. They brought their sons, Dave, Kenny and Gary. Gary was only a baby.

"Dan was a troubleshooter," said Sheldon (Shelly) Solow, a camper and counselor from 1964 to 1972. "He was an incredible magician. But what he really was, was a psychiatrist—he would sit and watch and figure out what made each kid tick."

"We had this kid in our cabin named Brian Maier who would have these night terrors. We called him Brian Nightmare," said Tod Himmel, a camper and counselor from 1969 to 1975. "Dan took him into his cabin, and we were all pretty sure he used hypnosis to cure him. He was very charismatic and a wonderful storyteller."

One summer, when camp spirit was low, Dan created a secret group called the Society of the Red Cones. There were no official rules, but there was a handshake and a password that only members knew. (Spoiler: It was "Ducksoup." Like the Marx Brothers movie.) It was under the radar and not

Dan Langell, the incomparable boys' program director from 1960 to 1974, talks with campers between innings. *Courtesy of Lake of the Woods and Greenwoods Camps.*

a part of any official camp program. There were just enough whispers about it that the kids all wanted in, even if they didn't know what it was. It was the perfect way to include the kids who were having a hard time adjusting to camp life. By the end of the summer, every kid was a member.

Dan didn't just work hard for the campers' sakes; he worked with his counselors, too. During pre-camp, the staff arrived a week early to set up their activities and undergo a crash course in summer camp counseling. Dan taught an incredible life lesson that every cabin had a leader. Every group had a leader. Sometimes there was a sub-leader or someone who wanted to be the leader. And the best way to run a cabin was to get the leader on your side.

"He came up to camp a couple of times in the mid-'80s while [his son] Dave was the program director and put on his magic show," said Jeff Miner, a counselor and boys' program director for thirteen years between 1984 and 2001. "It was really good, really funny. He taught me a lesson that I've never forgotten. These two kids walked up to him, and he had a ball of paper in his hand, and part of the trick was to throw the ball over the kids' heads to confuse them. I told him he should do that to a counselor, and he said, 'I'll never embarrass an adult I don't know in front of the kids they teach.'"

Laurie was a great camp director, and he saw how wonderful Dan was. Dan had an agenda and could be strict, but Laurie really let him run the camp as he saw fit. The same went for Lorraine at Lake of the Woods. "Lorraine was strict but very nice," said Linda Baskind Rosenberg, a camper and counselor from 1960 to 1969. "We were respectful of her." But in Lorraine's early summers, kids called her "Mother" behind her back. It was a teasing nickname with a hint of endearment.

Linda spent five years as a camper and five years as a counselor, with Lorraine always a presence. Linda's sister, Leslie, also went to Lake of the Woods. Years later, Linda sent her two boys, Jonathan and Michael, to Greenwoods, where they also became counselors. And she was great friends with Marc and Dave. The three of them were nearly inseparable.

With the staff and kids in the trusted hands of the Langells, Laurie could focus on the big picture, like recruiting, administration and creating the atmosphere he envisioned for the kids. His motto was "Strive for perfection, settle for excellence."

"One day, I was setting up the golf driving range," said Shelly. "Laurie came over from the Big House, and he starts giving me a hard time because two divider lines were slightly uneven. I told him, 'Strive for perfection, settle for excellence.' He laughed and walked back to the Big House."

And camp kept growing. As the two camps filled up, cabins had to be added to the boys' side. Numbers were always higher at Lake of the Woods, but Mrs. G. built such spacious cabins in 1952 that they held their own. One of the original cabins on the girls' side was lifted from where the Girls' Program Cabin is today and moved across the street and planted behind the modern-day Mohawk cabin. A shower was installed, and it became the boys' program director's cabin. As numbers fluctuated, that cabin alternated between being the program director's and being a proper cabin with counselors and kids, often called Cheyenne.

In 1963, a storage cabin was built outside the half-circle of cabins around the flagpole. Eventually, that cabin was outfitted with plumbing and was named Sioux. The current Mohawk cabin was built in 1966. Later, two tetherball courts were put up just outside Mohawk where younger kids could torture the oldest cabin forever more by playing early in the morning on Lazy Day. This is one reason the grundie hook came to be, but I'll get to that later. Two utilitarian cabins were built closer to Thunderbird Lodge. The one nearest was used as the rocketry activity cabin and the next as storage. But when camp really filled up and Cheyenne cabin was needed to house campers, half of the storage cabin was transformed into the program director's, complete with its own shower. Add the group shower house, and these twelve buildings remained this way, in purpose and style, for the next thirty years.

The cabin names and ages changed constantly on both sides of the road. This was especially so at Greenwoods because there were times when the youngest cabin only had six campers and certainly didn't require the larger buildings. The only cabins that have never changed names or ages are Chippewa and Barnard. Many of the names have lasted through the years. Some were retired, and one was removed following a minor drug scandal.

Potawatomi was a regular cabin name until 1972. By the early 1970s, the drug culture had made its mark on the youth culture. Even if kids weren't doing drugs, the awareness of them was, um, high.

"When I was in Potawatomi cabin in 1970, we had a chant that went, 'Smoke it up, toke it up, pot-pot-pot!'" Tod said. "And come on, if you looked at the sign, it kind of looked like it could be marijuana leaves."

There was a dramatic cultural shift in the 1960s. And this wasn't just a shift in camp culture. There was a sense of righteousness in America following

The defunct Potawatomi cabin in 1970. Tod Himmel was arguably the leading force behind the name's and sign's demise as he championed the Potawatomi chant, "Smoke it up, toke it up, pot, pot, pot." *Courtesy of Tod Himmel.*

World War II. The country was a leading world power, and the economy seemed invincible. The American Dream was not only propagated, but it was actually attainable for most hardworking citizens. There was a strange sort of social order to things. Perhaps it was the quiet fear instilled by the Cold War with the Soviet Union and the notion that a nuclear holocaust could occur at any moment that kept everyone in line. No matter, America was idyllic.

That changed in November 1963 when President John F. Kennedy was assassinated in Dallas, Texas. His murder turned the country on its side. Even though we had avoided nuclear war a year before, the president's death demonstrated that we were vulnerable. Television was the new medium, and we had more access to the ills of the world than ever. We couldn't just read and hear about them through newspapers and radio; we could actually *see* what was happening. And when Kennedy's accused killer was shot to death on live television that following Sunday morning, it was clear that the world was different.

Then the Beatles invaded America and changed rock-and-roll. Then the Rolling Stones came and changed it some more. Then the conflict in

Vietnam escalated, and the carnage was broadcast through living room boob tubes. The civil rights movement divided towns and changed demographics. Killing leaders was becoming routine and ghastly—Malcolm X, Martin Luther King Jr. and Robert Kennedy.

Even with all of this turmoil, summers at Lake of the Woods and Greenwoods still kept the kids in their own world—safe from all of it. But they came for a month or two after spending ten months among it. Tod remembered having boxing and wrestling night for evening program—kids put pillows over their hands and fought. "This was in 1970, at the height of pacifism," he said. "But we were fighting. Wasn't that ironic?"

"In the beginning [of camp], the kids had uniforms," Laurie said.

> *The advantage was that everyone was equal. There wasn't the problem of one girl having a designer pair of shorts versus the girl who had shorts from Sears. But people rebelled against that. I remember the first camper we got whose parents were getting divorced. That information may be on the* [camp] *application now. There's a family breakdown—a societal breakdown. The kids were better behaved, they minded their language better and they had a little more courtesy. All of that gradually disintegrated. It could be the influence of TV, a breakdown of the discipline in schools, who knows?*

The truth is, times change. Kids change. But the other truth is that kids don't change at all. They'll always be just kids.

Most kids, once they get a taste of it, want to spend their entire lives at camp. Marc Seeger had that opportunity. "I was six years old my first summer," he said. "I can still remember…It was very different. Like being in a different world."

Marc was a camper for ten years and then a counselor-in-training and a junior counselor; at nineteen, he was a full counselor. He took almost every activity camp offered. He was an incredible swimmer and a good shot with a rifle, earning his bar seven, which meant that he could shoot standing up. He loved sailing and liked water skiing but never went crazy for it like so many others. He was good at archery and enjoyed drama. Those drama classes paved the way for a lifelong interest in theater. He has since written and produced plays.

Marc was forced to learn horseback riding that first summer. He was about forty pounds, and his first time out the horse just kept bucking. He didn't go near a horse again for four years. He remembered the riding instructor that year sitting on the stoop of Chippewa cabin saying to him, "You're going to learn to like riding." And he did. Like the drama classes, this paid off in adult life, too. In 1997, there were problems with the riding staff, and no one was able to teach the classes. So, Marc strapped on his boots and taught riding for a week.

He took some time away from camp in the early 1970s to travel but came back to assist his father alongside his brother, Jerry. As the 1980s came on, Marc took on more leadership roles as the boys' program director in 1981 and co-assistant director with Jerry after that.

According to Marc, the hardest part of running a camp was hiring the staff. The staff had to be responsible, qualified and available for an entire summer. The maintenance staff was always first to arrive at camp, followed by the kitchen staff, the office staff, the counselors and then the nurses. In 1985, Marc hired the best nurse the camp ever saw and will ever see. It was a good thing, too, because 1985 was a medical nightmare.

Deb Bates had graduated nursing school that May. She was looking for jobs all over town in Grand Rapids, Michigan, but couldn't find a thing. She was a twenty-five-year-old single mom with twin seven-year-old boys to take care of. She needed a job and fast. She found an ad in a nursing magazine that a summer camp was hiring. She called Marc. Marc interviewed her. Marc didn't hire her.

Instead, he hired two nurses, neither of whom had young children to bring along as extra baggage. But for being medical professionals, these nurses didn't have very thick skin. They reported seeing a dead field mouse in the Infirmary when they arrived. Well, finding field mice around camp wasn't uncommon since it was surrounded by undisturbed farmland, a natural habitat for rodents. After these nurses made a scene about the mouse and prattled on about the unsanitary and unacceptable conditions, Marc had the mouse cleaned up. Problem solved. Or so he thought. The nurses hit the road in the middle of the night.

At breakfast the next morning, he asked the staff if anyone knew any available nurses. It was Friday. Camp started on Sunday. He was cutting it close. No one had any recommendations, so Marc headed back to the Big House and called Deb Bates—he needed her immediately. Deb still hadn't found a job, so she packed herself and her two boys, Dan and Doug, and headed to Decatur. Marc called another nurse named Katie whom he also didn't originally hire. She brought three kids with her.

The History of Lake of the Woods and Greenwoods Camps

"It was a disaster," Deb said of the Infirmary. "Nothing was organized or cleaned. I'm a big organizer and cleaner, so I started right away. Katie arrived a day later."

These were two young mothers making it up as they went along. Deb was fresh out of nursing school and wasn't scheduled to take her state boards until July. She was thrown into the job just before camp opened with the best of hopes. But it wasn't long before things got rocky. "We had head lice that year," Deb said.

> A good twenty or thirty girls had head lice. We had to send their laundry off to get a major boiling to kill it. The counselor Joe Trawinski suffered a head injury while skiing and needed stitches. A counselor needed treatment for poison ivy where the sun don't shine. Another got a call from his girlfriend at school, and he needed antibiotics for an STD. One kid dove into the lake and hit his head on the bottom. He came up with numbness. We had to take him to the hospital in Dowagiac. His dad was a neurosurgeon in Chicago, so…that was awkward.

"The Bryn Mawrs decided to get high. They took aspirin with Coke," Deb continued. There's an old wives' tale that ingesting these components will cause euphoria or act as an aphrodisiac. "Another camper reported it, and we had them take syrup of ipecac so they would vomit everything up." There's no truth at all to this idea. But Deb and Katie couldn't take the chances.

And then Katie got sick. "She was in the hospital for a while," said Deb. She contracted the Coxsackie A virus. Some of the campers had to be quarantined. Typically found in children, adults can catch it. It causes high fever, rash and blisters in the mouth and/or on the tonsils. With one nurse down, Deb was working at an alarming pace.

"A bunch of the counselors were going into town one night. I told Marc he was going to have to get someone to cover the Infirmary because I needed a night out and was going to the Penny Lane," a bar in town.

Call it kismet that the most famous of medical mishaps occurred that year. It's the event that left the biggest impact on campers and counselors and still resonates today: Bobby Goldwin getting hit by a car crossing 47th½ Street.

Bob was a camper and counselor from 1983 until 1993. He was well known as the cutest camper for several years, often attracting more attention from

The nurses of 1985 on opening day second session. *Left to right*: Deb and Katie. *Courtesy of Deb Bates.*

the Bryn Mawrs than any of the Mohawks could dream of. In 1985, Bobby was ten years old, in Sioux Cabin. It was the second week of camp, and he was walking back from dinner. He was on the Lake of the Woods side of the street when he saw Victor Perez, a junior counselor on the Greenwoods side.

"I saw that he was crossing, so I started crossing," Bob said. "I didn't bother to look both ways, I just looked at the counselor. Then he stopped and went back. And I looked." A car was barreling down the road, with Bobby standing in its crosshairs. There was little time to react, but Bobby jumped and slammed onto the hood of the automobile. His hat flew off his head; he bounced off the hood and landed on the ground. The driver of the car was the well-known bartender at the Penny Lane.

"I heard the screech of a car and saw the blur of a body. I remember thinking, 'God, I hope that's not Bobby,'" his older brother, Dan, said.

Bobby got up and started running around. He then ran to his brother and was taken to the Infirmary, where an ambulance rushed him to Borgess-Lee

Memorial Hospital in Dowagiac, a place quite familiar with the camp that summer. "I asked the paramedic, 'Are the sirens on?'" Bob said. "He said no. I said, 'I want my money back.'"

Other than a bruise the size of a small island on his leg, Bobby was fine. John Windomaker, a favorite counselor of both Goldwins, carried Bobby into the Mess Hall the next day to a standing ovation. "He milked it," Dan said. Their parents drove to camp from Indiana, and Bobby's father tried to convince Marc to post a sign nearby where his son was struck that would read, "Bobby Goldwin Pass." It never happened. What did happen after the accident was that a new job was created at Greenwoods Camp: the road guard.

Deb was such a star nurse in 1985 that she returned every summer for the next sixteen to train the camp nurses and help them through the hectic first day. "Camp was a wonderful experience for [my] boys, and most of the counselors were great role models for them," she said. "I remember going

Iroquois campers Dan and Doug Bates in 1985. Doug is the one with no shirt, while Dan is making the funny face. *Courtesy of Dan Bates.*

to the boys' camp when they were the youngest campers and watching them raise the flag in the morning. I was so proud of them. Since golf and the Riflery Range were right behind the Infirmary, they would stop by with their friends to get some bug juice or popsicles…Sometimes I wished I could have stayed through the summers."

For all of her behind-the-scenes influence, the legacy most people will remember her for are her twin boys, who went on to become two of Greenwoods' most well-liked campers and influential counselors.

Another challenge of directing the camp was dealing with the American Camping Association (ACA) inspectors. Lake of the Woods and Greenwoods never had a problem with the ACA, but Marc and Laurie had regular run-ins with one particular inspector who just liked to push their buttons.

During one visit standing in the Big House office, this inspector was pushing a few too many of Laurie's, though none that had anything to do with potential infractions or safety concerns. Laurie finally said, "Look! I wrote a book on camping. Would you like to read it?" Laurie grabbed the

Marc Seeger as a counselor spending some time with his campers, circa early '70s. *Courtesy of Lake of the Woods and Greenwoods Camps.*

A tug-of-war battle through the mud pit during a Greenwoods special day. *Courtesy of David Himmel.*

book from the shelf and shoved it in the inspector's face. It was a thick book. The inspector looked at it and read the cover: *What I Know About Camping*, by Lawrence Seeger. The inspector backed down and didn't bother the Seegers again. It was a good thing that he didn't call Laurie's bluff. That book was a joke—every page in it was blank.

It wasn't all headaches of course. Besides, the kids were always unaware of any problems rumbling through the Big House office. They were busy playing capture the flag and tree ball; having Cabin Night, the Vassar Mock Trial and Pow-Wow; and going on overnight camping trips and dunes trips. All of the headaches were sacrificial lambs for the kids' camp experience.

In 1985, Lake of the Woods Camp celebrated its fiftieth summer. The Seegers invited Mrs. G. to come up, and for the first time since 1956, she returned to the place she and her husband had built half a century earlier. Since then, she had undergone heart surgery and now walked with a cane, but she was still trucking along, as full of life as ever. Toba, Kenny, his daughter, Lois, her daughter and Ceil came with her. Laurie drove her around camp on the Seegermobile golf cart. She said that she felt like a princess.

Celebrating fifty years of Lake of the Woods Camp, July 1985. *Left to right*: Phyllis Seeger, Marc Seeger, Laurie Seeger, Florence Greenberg and Jerry Seeger. *Courtesy of Dan Bates.*

The flatbed trailer was brought down to the lake by the Archery Range, and a PA system was hooked up. Laurie and Jerry stood on the trailer and said a few things about Mrs. G. Laurie presented her with a bouquet of roses. She didn't stand on the trailer, but she kicked the cane and stood to talk about how the camp came to be and what a wonderful place it really was. Throughout the day, campers from the Greenberg era who made the pilgrimage kept saying to her, "Those summers were the best times of my life." And she liked that. She said, "The happiest days of my life were spent at camp with you kids. I'm going to spend the rest of the day in the clouds."

That was the last time Mrs. G. was at camp. She passed away two years later on June 25, a little more than a month shy of her ninetieth birthday.

Intermittently, between 1982 and 1988, all three Seeger men shared the title of owner/director. Laurie played the more distant role of the wise elder. He let his boys manage most things. He was there for pre-camp, opening and closing, Visitor's Day and, of course, for the fiftieth anniversary, but he was no longer in the trenches.

While the brothers loved each other, it was clear to the counselors and staff who knew them that working together put a strain on their relationship. They were like night and day, but they made it work. Jerry took care of the parents and kids, and Marc handled the operations.

"Jerry could be funny as hell," Miner said. "At one of the best staff training days I was ever a part of, Jerry was leading a discussion about something; I don't remember what it was or what he said, but he said something that had the entire staff laughing hysterically for two hours. He really could bring the funny." As personal as Jerry could be, Marc was the one you'd see walking around camp, taking kids out for a sail or on a trail ride, while Jerry hunkered down in the Big House.

In 1989, Marc officially bought the business from his father. There was no ceremonial passing of the torch, no weepy father/son moment where the boy is given the keys to the shop. It was a business transaction. And so, after thirty years of living the dream he had since he was twelve, Lawrence Seeger retired from the camping business. He went back to where he started and volunteered with the Boy Scouts of America. Now in his nineties, he still works closely with the Scouts and builds complete Native American ceremonial headdresses by hand for their programs.

Just before Marc bought the camp, Jerry got sick, too ill to run things alongside his brother. And he passed away a few years later. Then, the little homesick boy afraid of horses was a summer camp owner and director. It wasn't something Marc had dreamed of doing like his father had; it was the natural order of things. And because Marc had been assistant director and co-director for the last nine years, not much changed when he took the wheel.

"I'm all for tradition," he said. "We need it because we need bearings. The daily activities, making your own schedule and special days…I like that people came to camp for that. But the key thing is the relationships. Life is built on relationships, and that's what people *really* came back for, those relationships. It's like a tree. Each year the roots go deeper and deeper."

One particularly deep-rooted relationship was with a young former camper turned counselor named Dayna Glasson. Marc had bad luck with quality assistant directors. In 1991, he hired a former camp nurse named Dawn Barnard. He felt that her focus was elsewhere when it needed to be on the job. One way he described her was "man crazy." In the end, it was her professionalism that was her undoing.

Marc Seeger showing off the versatility of the Seegermobile, 1996. *Left to right*: GWC Dream Team waiters Anthony "Nicho" Nicholson, Ted Schmidt, Jeff Miner, Wayne Fleming, Jonathan Rosenberg and Ryan Wiedmayer. *Courtesy of Jeff Miner.*

During the sixth week of camp, Marc found a note on his desk from Dawn. It was a resignation letter. In it, she gave her two weeks' notice. For Marc, this was a dirty trick, a slap in the face. When the last day of camp came, Dawn was gone. No goodbyes. No "Can I help you with anything as the door hits my ass on the way out?" Just gone. He was left without an assistant director to help him with the end-of-the-season duties that were always plentiful. Dawn's leaving left him in a lurch. He needed to find someone he could depend on.

Dayna had spent several of her winter breaks from college helping Marc out in the office, as well as returning halfway through that summer to fill the void left by the firing of the girls' program director during the session changeover weekend. At the end of the summer, he offered her the job. He also threw more money at her than any assistant before. "I knew that having Dayna would mean we'd make that money back, and more. She was worth it," he said.

She accepted the job, and so Marc could once again focus on what he was best at, managing the details. Dayna was perfect for home visits and working with the parents and kids one on one. She had such a passion and talent for it all that she not only was assistant director but remained the program director as well. Additionally, the stress of hiring was off Marc's shoulders because he trusted Dayna to hire independently. She was the only person he trusted enough to do that, too. She stayed with Marc until the end of the summer in 1994, when she married and moved to Arizona.

Dayna's absence left room for a new assistant director, so camp had two years of Ean Cuthbert. And that was like having a collegiate male cheerleader with a chip on his shoulder bouncing around the Big House. Also new to the Big House was the Internet. The culture was shifting again because of the World Wide Web. "We went online in 1995," Marc said. "I saw the importance of it. And it was so much easier." Hiring was easier. Promotion was easier. And easier meant cheaper.

Still, the long days and late nights were taking their toll on Marc. "I don't think everyone knows the cost of being on the top," he said. "There are government regulations and parents and four or five kids that are really hard to handle. And that's what you end up dealing with, all the bad stuff."

Marc tried to get out of the Big House as often as he could and walk around to the different activities to spend time with the kids or even go for a swim, a sail or a ski. But those times were few and far between. And when they did occur, he felt the stress of what was waiting for him back at the office. By 1997, it was time for a change.

"It's a youthful-oriented business," Marc said. "My dad was in his mid-sixties when he left. But by fifty or fifty-five years old, it's time to hand over the reins." Marc was forty-seven years old when he made the phone call saying that he was ready to sell.

The Seegers owned Lake of the Woods and Greenwoods Camps for forty-two years. That's more than half as long as the camps have been in existence. They employed a cast of characters and gave a home for millions of memories for boys and girls the world over. They saw dramatic cultural changes occur in the outside world but maintained a state of sameness at camp. Laurie said, "It was like a play. The same script, different actors."

In 1977, Jimmy Buffett wrote a song originally intended for Elvis Presley to record. When Elvis died that year, Buffet recorded "Margaritaville" as his own. The song is a depressing tale of regret kept at bay by an alcoholic haze. It is still Buffett's biggest solo hit, and over the years, "Margaritaville" became less about the specific booze-fueled land of denial and instead about a place for easy living, good times, fine people and wonderfully warm weather.

A Staff Show performance of "Seegerville" in 1997. Marc Seeger is on the left in the hat. The original writer of the song, Jeff Miner, is standing behind Marc's left shoulder. *Courtesy of David Himmel.*

At the Staff Show in 1988, Navajo counselors Todd Lough, Miner and Brian Singer borrowed Buffett's tune to spoof the Lake of the Woods and Greenwoods experience.

"We sat down and did lyrics," Miner said. "Todd played guitar. We went over it a couple of times, and we were walking up the back steps of the rec lodge to do the song, and Todd said, 'Guys we gotta keep it slow, we gotta keep the tempo.' I said, 'Todd. I've heard the song five hundred times. Let's just sing it.'"

In that performance, the years between 1956 and 1997 were named and immortalized over and over again at Staff Shows with the camper favorite song, "Seegerville": "Wasting away again in Marc Seegerville. Searching for my lost camper or two."

Seegerville was a place out there away from everything. Troubles were no bother. Laurie and Marc created a utopia. They even created their own time zone. Seegertime was halfway between central and eastern time, used to adjust for daylight during the last two weeks of camp because that part of the country stays bright late. Today, they stop just short of denying that a Seegerville existed. They say that it was just a song. They don't realize the full impact they had all those years. Those who were there know that Seegerville was a place. And for many, it still is.

Chapter 5

CAMP FOOD

If kids don't eat and get big when they are little,
they will be little when they get big.
—*Mess Hall slogan*

First it was a dance hall and then a church. Eventually, it became a summer camp dining room and kitchen for Jewish kids. Although it was set at the far west corner of the property, it was the social hub where activity brewed and boiled over no matter what purpose it served. At one point in the early days, through the 1940s, there was stadium seating facing an adjoining outdoor theater. And while it has seen many redesigns, additions, demolitions and rebuildings, the Mess Hall remains today the hottest and loudest building in Decatur.

"The Mess Hall was the center of it all."
—*Tod Himmel*

The Mess Hall's slogan was shorthand for what an insistent mother would say: "Eat more! What do you want, you should grow up into a twig?" Early in the summers, Mrs. G. made an announcement proclaiming the high quality of food, noting that she only did dealings with the best purveyors and that if anyone had any complaints, they should speak up then. Only once did anyone say anything. It was her grandson, Kenny Neumann, being cute.

The History of Lake of the Woods and Greenwoods Camps

The original Mess Hall, with outdoor theater and bleachers, circa 1935. *Courtesy of Lake of the Woods and Greenwoods Camps.*

Greenwoods boys lined up under the Mess Hall slogan. Fourth in from the right is Kenny Neumann, Mrs. G.'s grandson. *Courtesy of Ceil Rothbart.*

Camp food was always held in high regard. The menu was eclectic, and the food was served family style. This gave way to perhaps the most enforced rule throughout camp: You kill it, you fill it.

A Camp Story

For decades, before the original Mess Hall was revamped in 2004, every table had a red X painted on two opposing diagonal corners. These Xs were the hopper spots. Most often, this determined who would clear the table after each meal. Campers rotated either every meal or every day around the table so that each of them would get the responsibility. Counselors were pardoned from the rotation and always sat in the chairs at the ends of the table. But if only one counselor was at the table, the day that a camper rotated into the other chair was a great day indeed. Because, come on…you were in the *chair*.

The Xs were really just there for guidance. Dining was democratic. The rules of the table were created and enforced by those sitting at the table. There were times when table clearers were determined by games. The counselors might, at some point during the meal, place their fingers on their noses. This was done coyly, not to draw attention. The last two campers to repeat the gesture were responsible for clearing. And it didn't always have to be a finger to the nose. It could have been a thumb on the table or a thumb in the middle of the forehead, with the remaining fingers spiked into the air.

The Greenwoods side of the Mess Hall in the early 1960s. *Courtesy of Lake of the Woods and Greenwoods Camps.*

Sometimes this game was done to determine the person who would get more food when something ran out. Or that was left to the hoppers on the X. But most commonly, whomever killed it had to fill it.

What this meant was that if someone took the last of something and didn't leave enough for at least one more serving, that person had to get a refill. This was easily determined when dealing with food like French toast or grilled cheese. It often sparked debate with items like soup. "There's plenty there for another bowl," one might say. To settle the dispute, the remaining soup was ladled out, and a verdict was made.

Of course, before any food could be served and any table cleared, tables had to be set. This was the job of one particular cabin for one day. Program directors determined the schedule. And fifteen minutes before each meal, table setters would be called over the camp's PA system. The OD (or on-duty) counselors escorted the cabin to the Mess Hall and oversaw the process. ODs also stayed behind to observe and release the table clearers once their job was done to the satisfaction of that counselor.

Being a table setter was awful. It cut into playtime. However, it did provide an opportunity for debauchery. Being in the Mess Hall before any other cabin was prime for setting booby traps like loosening the caps on

---

How to Spike a Cup

1. *Quickly jam a fork into the center of the cup causing at least two puncture holes.**
2. *Wait for the unsuspecting camper or counselor (if you dared) to pour a beverage.*
3. *Laugh at their realization that the contents of the cup are on the table, on their shirt or in their lap.*
4. *Deny any involvement in the prank.*
5. *Find a scapegoat to be punished and forced to clean the table's mess.*

*You can also remove the paper cone cup from its holder and tear the paper away at the tip.

---

the sugar, salt or pepper shakers so when a hapless camper or counselor went to add seasoning to the food, a pile of flavor ended up on the plate and likely all over the table. But the greatest Mess Hall prank of all was spiking the cup.

Several generations of campers drank their bug juice from paper cone cups that sat in plastic holders. These were easily pierced with a fork, which often ended in a mess, stained clothes and hilarity. But these cups were also an unintentional enemy on cold mornings when hot chocolate was served. If you didn't layer two or three cups in your cup holder, the heat would release the glue holding the cone together and things would end with a mess, stained clothes and a scalding. And hilarity. It was about 2000 when Styrofoam cups were served with the hot chocolate and not just hoarded by counselors for their coffee.

In 1991, when I was in Comanche cabin, we prided ourselves on being wretched little troublemakers. We routinely set the cabin floor on fire by spraying our names in bug spray and lighting it. Ryan Kessler, Brett Katz and cousin Richie Katz snuck out, hijacked the Seegermobile and crashed

Do these boys look like shameless, sadistic pyromaniacs? Because they were. *Courtesy of David Himmel.*

it into a power box, which knocked out electricity to the camp, as well as to the Timber Trails RV Park. We were prepubescent rebels without a cause. So, as table setters, we thought it was funny to spike the cups at the staff table. Several of us took forks and leisurely walked around the table, swiftly stabbing each cup at every place setting. In hindsight, it was a pretty stupid thing to do since it was clear that the table setters were the culprits. We had to clear the staff table for a week. I'm not going to admit that I was one of the kids who did the spiking. But I won't deny it. And it could have been my idea. But it also could not have been.

There were a few simple rules everyone could follow to ensure a clean and healthy camp life: hang up any wet items on the cabin hooks to dry, sweep under the bed to eradicate earwigs and always, always, *always* check your cup before pouring anything.

For a good stretch from the late 1990s to the mid-2000s, cup spiking was impossible. The new owner, Dayna Hardin (née Glasson), got rid of the old paper cone cups and cup holders and replaced them with hard plastic juice cups like you might see at a roadside diner. However, by 2011, spiking was back when the diner juice cups were replaced with clear plastic Solo cups. The only drawback to these was that unlike their paper ancestors, they were unable to hide their holes. But that doesn't stop campers from making the effort.

> *"There was always peanut butter and jelly on the tables."*
> —*Roselle Redman Hechter*

Although the menu was diverse and kept the majority of the campers and staff nourished and happy, some people were just picky eaters. Thankfully, there was peanut butter and jelly and a basket of white or wheat bread for sandwiches at every meal. Some would forego all reason and instead make a butter and sugar sandwich—just two pieces of bread smothered in butter and caked in sugar. A complete diabetic snack.

Today, due to the increase in food allergies to peanuts or other tree nuts, you won't find peanut butter and jelly on the tables. In fact, you won't find peanut anything anywhere in camp. And that has affected the Canteen as well. Even candy that doesn't contain peanuts, like plain M&M's, aren't served because they're made in the same factory as peanut

M&M's, Snickers and other nutty candies, and so contamination is a risk. The old mason jars of peanut butter have been replaced with jars of Kraft Jet-Puffed Marshmallow Crème. Surprisingly, marshmallow fluff is quite nutritious and makes a sweeter, if unorthodox, replacement to the favorite American sandwich.

Since I'm mentioning flavorful spreads, it would be a disservice if Vegemite weren't included here. Camp provided many opportunities to not just befriend foreign campers and counselors but to also learn a little about other countries. And although the foreign staff was made up of Brits, Swedes, Germans, Canadians, Mexicans, Israelis, Kiwis and so on, it was likely the Australians who made the most lasting cultural impact on the American boys and girls. And that's due to Vegemite. It's a good thing many of those Aussies were likeable blokes and sheilas because otherwise the Aussies would have left an awful taste in many of the Americans' mouths.

"Vegemite is a staple in another country that probably will never catch on in the United States," said Billy Hearth, a counselor from 1996 to 1998 and the boys' program director in 1999. "I think it's horrendous. It's a flavor that is indescribable. You have to taste it to understand it. You…you just have to taste it. Food transcends boundaries. It tells you about the people and about their culture. I think food is an important makeup of who we are. It tells me that Australians are gritty. Not in a bad way. No, not at all. But to be able to eat that and enjoy it as a staple…it's beyond me."

Vegemite is yeast extract. It has an extremely salty taste, so a little goes a long way. It's a fantastic source of vitamin B, and like the marshmallow fluff, Vegemite is a Kraft product. It is the peanut butter and jelly of Australia. And much of Australia's view of peanut butter and jelly is no different than ours of Vegemite.

Anthony "Nicho" Nicholson, an Australian living in Woodonga, Victoria, was the Greenwoods tripper from 1996 to 1999. He was also the assistant program director alongside Billy in '99. "Peanut butter. What is it about you Americans and your infatuation with peanut butter and jelly?" he began.

For starters, America is the only nation in the western world that calls jam "jelly." Wouldn't you think that as with the other civilized nations, jelly would be the product that derives from jelly crystals? While jam is a product of the fruits it is derived from like apricot, marmalade, strawberry.

This aside, jam—jelly, whatever you want to call it—what are Americans thinking? If ever two products were not meant to be together, here they are. It ain't no Abbott and Costello, no Beavis and Butthead, no Bella and Edward…But hey, it is as American cliché as baseball and Starbucks. And still, we do love those American clichés. So I suppose we will just have to accept the weird combinations and bizarre product names you use. We are happy to stick with our Kangaroo Pies and Crocodile steaks.

Aussies would bring their own jars of Vegemite with them. Big jars, too. As part of the Greenwoods What About Bob evening activity, campers were challenged to eat a saltine cracker with Vegemite spread and then whistle. The challenge was less the whistling with a dry, salted mouth from the cracker and more about not gagging on the taste of the spread.

I, however, love the stuff. It took me ten years, but I genuinely love it. When I told Nicho that peanut butter was outlawed at camp and replaced with marshmallow fluff, he sat quietly for a moment then said, "It is a world gone mad."

Through the years, favorite meals have remained constant among the majority of camp diners. Those meals were spaghetti, Al's fried chicken, tacos, grilled cheese sandwiches and tomato soup, the outdoor barbecue on special days and the individual cabin Sunday night cookout.

Being a cook was hard work. Mary Jernagin was a cook in 1973. She worked for the Chicago Board of Education in food service during the year, so with summers off, cooking in the Mess Hall was a perfect job. Mary lived in Chicago's South Side when Laurie hired her. Unfortunately, she had to stay home after that first summer for the next six years and mind her children because she said they were acting up and she needed to be there to keep them in line. She happily returned in 1979, with her children grown and well behaved, and stayed until 1987, when she became head cook from '88 until '90.

> *"Even though I totally remember burning my thumb on the metal hot dog holders, the cookout was my favorite meal. I switched to sticks after being burned."*
> —Stacey Jacobson, camper
> *1994–96*

During her time at camp, Mary was part of a recurring three-person dream team consisting of herself, Head Cook Al Lewis and Head Baker Lola Johnson. "Even though [we all] worked for the school board, we didn't get a chance to see each other during the school year," Mary said. "But in the summer, we just got right back into it. There were three adults, and the rest were foreign kids. They were good college kids, they were all goodhearted people."

With a complete staff of seven, routinely "five boys and two girls," Mary said that they all helped one another out. So, on days Lola didn't have to bake, she would help cook. "The kitchen was always working together. There was order to the chaos."

The days were long. There were early mornings to prep breakfast. Then it was right into lunch and on to making dinner. Once dinner was over with, it was time to clean it up so they could do it all over again. Mary said that the days of the big barbecues were the longest. She wasn't quite an old lady, but the hard work, even though she loved it, wore her out. She spent her days off sleeping. She had her own cabin, and those college kids on the staff would bring her breakfast, lunch and dinner so she could rest up.

> "The barbecue chicken and corn on the cob we ate outside of the Mess Hall was my favorite meal. Then you had Lola sitting by the popsicle cooler taking tickets and giving out pudding pops."
> –Bob Goldwin

Mary would have stayed at camp forever, but her grandson was killed in 1990, and she just never came back to orchestrate another barbecue. She still lives in the South Side and regularly thinks fondly of her summers in Decatur. "Everyone was so nice. It was like a vacation with pay. And I enjoyed every minute of it."

The food was good. All of it. Even the cold cuts, a lunch meal that was never a favorite of anyone's, weren't terrible. "I ate twenty fish sticks in one sitting," said Dan. Similarly, as a camper, I enjoyed a record of twenty bowls of Lucky Charms in one breakfast sitting. Sure, Lucky Charms isn't a camp food, but like Dan, it was a gluttonous task.

Still, not to be outdone, Dan witnessed a kid two years older than him snort lines of grated parmesan cheese. "Someone told him that if you snort the cheese, you would get high the same way you would if you snorted cocaine," Dan said. "He did a lot of parmesan cheese."

Vegemite may have created a cultural divide between campers and staff, but when the cooks in the kitchen delivered a favorite meal, everyone put down their butter knives and joined in the demanding chant of a cook's parade. Sung to the tune of "The Farmer in the Dell," the song could be started by anyone, but like most songs in the Mess Hall, the older cabins usually took the initiative:

We want a cook's parade!
We want a cook's parade!
Hi-ho, the derry-o,
We want a cook's parade!

The tune was repeated until the entire kitchen staff stopped what they were doing and came into the dining area to make a small parade to the center of the room, where they received an incredible standing ovation. It lasted until they returned back to work to the continued hoots and hollers.

While a cook's parade was not a regular occurrence, reserved for only the best meals, two particular menu items brought out the best of cook's parade cheers. The first was Al's fried chicken. Al was the head cook at camp from 1962 to 1981. "Oh, he just loved that camp," Mary said. "He thought the place was his." Beloved by his staff of foreign college kids, Lola and Mary, as well as every camper and counselor who ate even one bite of his camp food, Al had a stroke in the winter of 1981, making him unable to return to his camp. However, his legendary fried chicken lived on. It was so popular that Dan and Doug remember eating Al's fried chicken during their first couple of years at camp—even though they didn't start going until 1985, four years after Al was there. What they were eating was Mary's version of Al's fried chicken. As it was, no matter who fried the bird, if it was made in the Mess Hall, it was Al's.

The second favorite item—and only because dessert comes last—was Lola's apple crisp. Whenever apple crisp was served, Lola received her own slow chant from the campers and staff of "Low-lah…Low-lah…" until she came out and accepted her praise. In fact, outside of Color Days, there may have been nothing else that campers got more excited about.

> *"Lola's apple crisp. One of the best things I've ever had."*
> *—Rory Zacher, camper/counselor 1989–94, 1998*
>
> *"I hated Lola's apple crisp. I just don't like baked fruit."*
> *—Dan Goldwin*

Today, the Mess Hall still buzzes with activity, so in that respect it's no different than it was in 1935. But today's Mess Hall is a giant in comparison. It had to be built to accommodate the increasing number of campers and staff calling camp home each summer. All that remains of the original Mess Hall is the main dining room, though it's tough to recognize with all of the additions built around it. In 2005, there were new camps to feed. The Grove and The Glen were full of hungry kids and staff, too.

With the new Mess Hall came more square footage in the dining areas, as well as a larger kitchen for the twenty-two members of the kitchen staff—a number that makes Mary recoil in amazement. There is an annex just off where the staff table is located that is home to two complete salad and pasta bars. Color Days plaques and flags still adorn the walls, with plenty of room for the coming years.

In an effort to keep gum from making its way to the bottoms of tables and chairs, and on the Mess Hall floor, gum trees located at the Lake of the Woods and Greenwoods entrances were designated as the place to stick gum before coming in to dine. There was also one additional gum tree that remains near the Girls' Program Cabin. When the new Mess Hall was built,

The modern-day Mess Hall looking toward the Lake of the Woods side of the dining room. *Courtesy of David Himmel.*

Lake of the Woods entrance to the old Mess Hall. The gum tree is in the foreground on the left. *Courtesy of Lake of the Woods and Greenwoods Camps.*

the original gum trees were sacrificed, but a new tree has been anointed for the camps to share.

Those old gum trees were works of art. To put your chew on the trees was an exercise in impressionism and in abstract, renaissance or baroque styles of expression. Rough, wooden canvases with names written in bright pink and fluorescent chicle, massive and miniature blobs of flavor pushed into the cracks and crevasses.

"Camp was the theme of my Bat Mitzvah. The gum tree was one of the tables. I kept the centerpiece for years."
        —Lindsay Saewitz, camper/counselor 1991–2002

"How cool is it that I wrote my name in gum?"
        —Melissa Parker, camper 1992–96

"On my first day at camp, when I was walking to my cabin, I walked past the gum tree [near the program cabin] and was so fascinated by it that I almost bumped right into it. Ever since then, I have always been careful when walking past it," said Amy Werner, who has attended as a camper and counselor since 2003. "When I was in Vassar cabin, the girls in my cabin would blow bubbles with their gum and then stick them on the tree. The bubbles would sometimes last for a few days, and we would have competitions to see which bubble would last the longest." There were other competitions. Campers climbed counselors' shoulders to stick their Bubble Yum higher than anyone else had and approached the trees with an eye on the current record-holding wad.

They were like Western Walls for summer camp. Every piece of gum that adorned the bark came with a tiny prayer—intentional or otherwise—asking for a tasty meal or, more often, that it would remain the biggest wad, sturdiest bubble, most stretched-out design or highest-placed piece of gum for eternity.

> *"We used to tell the younger campers not to touch the gum tree or you would get 'Linky Con-Punky!' They'd ask what that was and we'd break into some funky dance and hip-hop tune about touching the gum tree and getting 'Linky Con-Punky!'"*
> —*Aaron "Quiz" Quisenberry,*
> *counselor/assistant boys' program director 1993–94*

In 2009, a gum tree epidemic was narrowly averted. Many younger Lake of the Woods girls wanted to make their own gum tree, and pieces of sticky gum started showing up randomly throughout camp. "The situation is much more under control, but I still warn my campers to look before they lean against a tree," said Amy.

Looking at a gum tree was like looking into the past. Much like reading the names inside of the dressers or on the walls and ceiling of the Girls' Program Cabin or in the ski shed and sailing cabinet, the pieces of gum were marks of proof that someone was there.

The Mess Hall is more different today than ever. But if there's one thing that's sure, it's that camp food is good. Always has been. Always will be. Even without peanut butter.

CANTEEN

Canteen is where campers and counselors can buy sundries like bug spray, ponchos, deodorant, toothpaste and other like items. But that was not as important as what Canteen means to their blood sugar. Canteen, especially for the younger cabins, was where the day began and ended. Some kids would have given their kingdom for Half-Canteen. It could be used to bribe or threaten kids with punishment. The campers used it as a barter system. Something like, "Lemme play on your Game Boy during rest hour, and I'll give you Half-Canteen tomorrow," or, "Make my bed" or "Lemme see your *Playboy*."

"I want the candy."

"I'll give you the ice cream or pop."

"I want the candy."

"Fine. But I get your Game Boy and your *Playboy* at rest hour and fifth period."

For a while, Canteen was after evening program, but when it was moved to after lunch, kids sprinted from the Mess Hall to get in line for their treats. Once through the door, which always took *forever*, a camper was allowed two items. One could be a candy bar, the other an ice cream cone, freeze pop or other frozen delight, or a bag of popcorn or a cup of soda. Sometimes kids tried to pass off a package of Reese's Peanut Butter Cups from the freezer as ice cream instead of candy so they could have two candy bars. A moot discussion would take place between that camper and the office staffer charged with running Canteen, who, despite the children's best arguments, would not allow them to get both the frozen Reese's and a bag of M&M's. There was just no tricking the Canteen overlord. This was, of course, when peanut-based candies were still permitted at camp.

Canteen order for the boys and the girls was determined by the program director and usually organized by cabins. Sometimes it was done by height. But that created a new problem where kids were measuring themselves and overstretching or standing on tippy toes in order to get ahead in line. Some were known to put rocks in their shoes to add lift. If it happened to be shortest to tallest, kids would hunch their shoulders or slightly bend their knees—anything to get into the Canteen sooner. Cabin cleanup inspection scores could also determine Canteen order. Because Canteen was so important to the kids, this ensured a sparkling-clean camp. At times, the kids would go so overboard in an effort to get a high score that they swept the outside of the cabin. Yeah, they swept the dirt. And just for fun, in what could be considered an abuse of power, the Canteen order would be the score of cabin cleanup from lowest to highest. This was met with loud groans and protests from the kids.

For many years, the boys' and girls' Canteens were separate. Lake of the Woods always used the Big House store. The original boys' Canteen was inside of the Boys' Rec Lodge in the back corner attached to the back of the program cabin. It hasn't been used for that purpose since the late 1970s, but it's still there as storage for toilet paper and contraband. It has a hinged, wooden window that was pulled up and opened by a string and pulley system. As always, responsible and entertaining campers manned it.

In the early 1970s, Tod and his good pals Danny Projansky, Gerry Berlin and Mike Shapiro made up songs for every item anyone ordered and lifted the window singing the *Bugs Bunny Show* theme song, "This Is It":

Overture, curtain, lights
This is it, the night of nights
No more rehearsing and nursing a part
We know every part by heart
Overture, curtains, lights
This is it, we'll hit the heights
And oh what heights we'll hit
On with the show this is it
Tonight what heights we'll hit
On with the show this is it

But when it moved to the Big House, a new challenge arose. Boys weren't allowed to bring their goods across the road into the cabin area. There was concern that food in the cabins would attract mice. However, every boy at Greenwoods knew that at least one person in each cabin had a stash of snacks. The most common in the last three decades were cans of Pringles potato chips. The plastic lids made sure that the chips stayed fresh and crisp in the humidity, as well as deterred any vermin looking for a bite.

Because bringing candy across the road was forbidden, it had to be done. The road guard was on post not only to keep kids from pulling a Bobby Goldwin but also to prevent food from crossing the street. He was a modern-day TSA agent. In fact, the TSA probably took many of its airport security tactics from the road guard manual.

The road guard frisked every kid who crossed. Boys hid candy in the waistbands of their shorts, down their underpants—front and back. They tucked candy bars under their hats and in their armpits, any place they could think of. If kids did manage to get candy across, their Charleston Chew tasted a little like underpants.

Others walked behind the Infirmary and threw their candy across the road to the baseball diamond, got patted down by the road guard, crossed and then made a mad dash for their booty waiting in the grass just over the wooden fence along the third base line. If the road guard or any other counselor saw this, that kid likely lost Canteen the next day. And that might as well have been a death sentence.

Losing Canteen was the ultimate punishment. And it could be revoked for any number of infractions. Ditch class? Lose one Canteen. Keep talking during flag? Lose another Canteen. Curse loudly in front of a camp director? Canteen. Gone. If the cabin as a whole was acting out, the lot lost Canteen.

The citizen's arrest allowed one kid to claim the Canteen of another. In an effort to keep the camp free of litter, the citizen's arrest rule was upheld:

> Should Camper A leave his or her candy wrapper on the ground, or anywhere but in the designated trash receptacles, Camper B may then pick up that trash, hold it high above the head and exclaim, "Citizen's arrest!" Camper B, along with witnesses, can report Camper A to the nearest counselor, earning Camper B one free Half-Canteen at the cost of Camper A. Camper B has the choice of the item, which means he or she can have two pieces of candy on one day.

Because the reward for a citizen's arrest was so attractive, some kids acted like narcs, waiting for someone to drop a piece of trash so they could swoop in and claim it as litter before the other could lean down to pick it up. It was like Decatur's own little Environmental Protection Agency. But really, it was an accidental good deed in an effort to get more of that sweet sugar high.

Chapter 6

MISS LOLA

I may not know your name, but I know your eyes.
—Lola Mae Johnson

Lola's apple crisp almost never made it to camp, because Lola almost never worked there.

Lola Mae Johnson lived in the South Side of Chicago most of her life in an apron and surrounded by children. She applied for the baker position in 1976. Laurie didn't hire her at first, a would-be major mistake but one he luckily avoided. Just before camp opened, Laurie found himself in need of a baker when the one he did hire fell through. He called Lola. She went on to be the longest-lasting employee at the camp, working there for more than twenty-five consecutive years.

Over those years, Lola became like an omnipotent shaman. Like Yoda. She was born in 1925. And though she was only in her late seventies during her final summer in 2001, she was always seen as the old baker with the waddle in her walk who oozed wisdom. To solidify this image, she began getting invited to speak at the nondenominational Saturday night services starting in about 1998.

Each week, services had a different theme. One would be about nature, the next about making the most of your time at camp and other like themes. Lola's gig was about brotherhood and sisterhood. And as she made her way in the golf cart down to the waterfront where services took place, at the hill of the Archery Range, campers and counselors received her with applause and cheers. She stood, leaned on her cane

THE BAKER		APPLE CRISP		CARD B – 7.11	
Yield: 2 – 18" x 26" x 1" Pans Cut 10 x 7				Oven Temp: 375° F Oven Time: 40 min.	

INGREDIENTS	WEIGHTS	MEASURES	FOR PORTIONS	PROCEDURE
Apples (Canned)	....	3 – #10 cans	....	1. Arrange 4½ qts. of apples in each
Lemon Juice	....	½ cup		greased pan.
Lemon Rind (Grated)	....	1 tbsp.	....	2. Sprinkle lemon juice and grated
Granulated Sugar	2 lbs. 12 oz. ..	1½ qts.	....	lemon rind over the apples.
Instant Thickener	4 oz.	⅞ cup		
Cinnamon (Ground)	....	3 tbsp.	....	3. Combine dry ingredients; sprinkle
Salt	....	1 tbsp.	....	over apples in each pan.
TOPPING:				
Brown Sugar	3 lbs.	2 qts.	....	1. Combine ingredients; blend to
Flour	2 lbs.	2 qts.		form a crumbly mixture. Sprinkle
Baking Powder	....	1-2/3 tsp.		half the mixture evenly over the
Baking Soda	....	1¾ tsp.	....	apples in each pan.
Salt	....	1 tbsp.	....	2. Bake until top is browned.
Butter (Soft)	2 lbs.	1 qt.	....	

VARIATIONS: 1. For a CHEESE APPLE CRISP, add 1 lb. (1 qt.) of grated cheddar cheese to the flour-sugar mixture in TOPPING step No. 1.
2. For a CRUNCHY APPLE CRISP, add 1 lb. 4 oz. (2 qt.) of rolled oats and reduce the flour to 1 lb. 4 oz. (1¼ qts.) in TOPPING step No. 1.

CHICAGO BOARD OF EDUCATION — BUREAU OF LUNCHROOMS

Lola's apple crisp recipe. However, it is missing one secret ingredient. *Courtesy of Chicago Board of Education—Bureau of Lunchrooms and Lake of the Woods and Greenwoods Camps.*

and preached what she knew about the camp connection and how we were all family—in it together.

Lola had a way of saying things that carried a great importance. If Lola said it, then it must have been so. She was loyal and fair. She never feigned knowing a camper or counselor and was often heard saying, "I may not know your name, but I know your eyes."

At a kitchen staff meeting her first summer in '76, Laurie said, "If I say make mosquito soup, you make mosquito soup." And Lola repeated the line back to him throughout his years as her boss when he gave her any direction.

"Yes, Mr. Seegum. 'If you say make mosquito soup, I'll make mosquito soup.'" That's what she called Laurie. Always Mr. Seegum. And he knew that she would do whatever she needed to do, however she needed to do it, to keep him happy, which was keeping the kids happy. And he respected her because of it. Marc respected Lola as well. And that respect saved my ass.

In 1993, I was nearly kicked out of camp. During my junior Mohawk year, I snuck out with Kessler, who was my lower bunkmate and best pal, and Josh Dritz, a friend in Navajo cabin. We made it to the Mess Hall to meet some girls, though they didn't leave enough of an impact on us that we can recall them now. The few of us were hanging out back in the kitchen, eating cake left over from dinner out of the staff refrigerator, when I decided that it would be funny to play with the fire extinguisher. So I took it off the wall, pulled the pin and squeezed the handle.

A cloud of white chemicals burst out of the nozzle covering the stovetop, ovens, baking equipment and pretty much everything in a ten-foot radius. I laughed. Kessler laughed. Dritz laughed. The girls laughed. Then we ran.

I don't know how we were found out, but the next day we were on the Big House porch. Marc was ready to send us home. And I felt awful. Forget getting kicked out; I felt awful because I did something really stupid that screwed over a lot of people. The chemicals on the equipment prevented a hot breakfast for the entire camp and cost Marc who knows how much in cleanup. I didn't know there were poisonous chemicals in a fire extinguisher. I was fourteen. I guess I thought water would shoot out. I'd never used a fire extinguisher or even seen one used. I was an idiot.

And what if I had been kicked out? What would have become of me? I might have grown up to become a lobbyist, or worse, a successful lobbyist. Lola saved me. She told Marc, "Don't send them boys home, Marc. They was just bein' mischievous. They don't mean no harm."

At dinner that night, we had to apologize to the entire camp. The three of us boys spent the next day doing manual labor with the maintenance staff. We hauled a lot of trash around camp that day and dug the tug-of-war pit in Campcraft. Basically, we did the work of an Arrowhead, something I was never awarded. Shooting the fire extinguisher off may have been the reason.

Lola taught me forgiveness that day. She taught me that sometimes people do bad things but don't mean "no harm." And sometimes they should be forgiven. Marc doesn't remember this happening. But I'll never forget it.

In 1999, I was the waterfront director and sailing instructor. That year, thanks to Dayna and the company charge card, the Sail Dock was ripe with three new Sunfish sailboats and a Hobie Cat. I named one of the Sunfish *Lola Mae*. When I took Dayna's golf cart to the Mess Hall to get Lola and bring her down to the dock for the ceremony and a few photos, we talked about the fire extinguisher incident. She remembered it and retold her side of it the same exact way she had told it to me six years earlier when I went to thank her for defending me.

"Marc wanted to send you boys home," she said. "But I knew you then. I didn't know your name, but I knew your eyes. And your eyes weren't bad. You weren't meanin' anybody no harm. You was just a mischievous boy. But I know you now, David. You've come a long way. But you still a little

Camp Baker Lola Johnson, with sailing instructor David Himmel at the 1999 dedication of the new *Lola Mae* sailboat. *Courtesy of David Himmel.*

mischievous, ain't you? I know. But you a good young man now. I know your eyes, David."

In 1996, the kitchen was becoming a little worse for the wear. Marc told Lola, "I have a surprise for you." He showed her the new refrigerators he had installed, and she cried. The refrigerators weren't just out of necessity; they were his gift to her.

"She was always so hard to stay in touch with. But I'd get a hold of her every year around January," said Dayna.

I wanted to be sure she was coming back, and every year it was the same conversation. She'd say, "You know if these knees don't give out between now and June, I'll be there no matter what." I'd hold my breath until she finally pulled into camp. She'd get out of the car and say, "Thank God my knees are still good that I can do this job."

At the end of the summer, I'd send a lot of the leftover food home with her. She'd pull away with her car stuffed to the hilt with number 10 cans of tomatoes. You couldn't see anything out of the back window.

I cried every time they cheered for her. Every single time, for twenty years, I cried. Here's this old baker, who could barely bake like she used to, and they were cheering. Having Lola at camp, I felt protected. I felt that we were all protected. She would say, "I ask God to watch over us. I ask God to watch over this kitchen."

In 2009, a stray black dog showed up at camp. Specifically, it showed up at the Mess Hall for every meal and was only seen around the Mess Hall. Associate Director Dana "DC" Cohn named the dog Lola. It was fitting. Office Manager Keeley Finnegan saw that Lola the dog received the proper shots, and that summer, the Mess Hall had a mascot. At the end of the season, she was taken to a no-kill shelter. "I hope she's with a good family," DC said.

How many of us can still taste her apple crisp melting in our mouths, the sugar covering our teeth like little sweaters? How many of us can still smell her dinner rolls being pulled from the oven and thrown into serving bowls as we said grace? How many of us remember her slouched in her plastic chair

Pals David Himmel and Lola Johnson having a drink and laugh at the 1999 all-staff dinner. *Courtesy of David Himmel.*

at the outdoor barbecues saying, "You can only have one ice cream. I don't care whose ticket you got. I know you been here." She was always looking after us. And though her apple crisp may have suggested otherwise, she was looking after our sugar intake, too.

She was slow to respond to the chants. It was those darn knees. But she'd make her way out from behind the counter with a slightly crooked smile below those thick glasses. Then she'd shuffle back to the kitchen. She knew we loved her.

Lola and Mary were great friends. She tried to keep contact with Lola, but it proved difficult. I called her once, years ago, over the winter. Someone picked up, a kid. I asked to speak to Lola. I was told to hold on. There was a lot of the kid's yelling on the other end before I was disconnected. Mary only has a phone number for Lola's sister, who doesn't return messages. The last that Mary heard, Lola was living in Georgia with her son. Laurie and Marc spoke with her on the phone while she was in a nursing home in a Georgia suburb in March 2011. All attempts to reach her since have been fruitless.

I feel sorry for the kids and staff who never met her or enjoyed her baking talents. I'm sure these people tire of hearing the rest of us drone on about it. I consider myself lucky to have had a personal relationship with her. And I know that even if someone never said one word to her, they knew there was something special about that lady. And she knew that there was something special about that person, too. There had to be. That's what brotherhood and sisterhood was all about.

If we all head up to the Mess Hall and start chanting her name, maybe she'll show up. If not from behind the kitchen counter, then from behind our eyes. These eyes she knew so well.

Chapter 7

THIS IS NOT A COED CAMP

And we'll soothe the forever boys and girls and before we're through, we'll find a name for this dern golden eternity and tell a story, too.
—Jack Kerouac

Hormones are tricky. They can be terrible wardens of social awkwardness, protruding acne and body shapes that would make Euclid of Alexandria scratch his head in geometric wonder. But hormones can also be the gentle guardians of first love, a flattering smile among the braces and, if you're lucky, a body that looks halfway human in a bathing suit. And it seems that hormones' busy season is summertime.

"This is not a coed camp" are words that have been said by nearly every director, assistant director and program director who ever worked at Lake of the Woods and Greenwoods. And it's a lie. Ask Dayna about Sam Sezati, her boyfriend when she was in Bryn Mawr. He still has a purple bandana she gave him. And that was more than twenty-five years ago. Let's remember that the first two summers the camp was in existence, it was unquestionably a coed camp under one name. Being a coed camp is a seventy-eight-year-old tradition.

But the directors had to say things like that. If they didn't, imagine the chaos of three hundred or more wound-up boys and girls clamoring for the attention of one another. It would be a nonstop awkward orgy of shy flirting and peacock showmanship. When young people are in love, or just in the mood, they can't be stopped. But they can be restrained. And the directors knew this. That's why there were dances and coed special

The History of Lake of the Woods and Greenwoods Camps

Not a coed camp, eh? A social inside Louis Lodge, circa 1950. Note the girls wearing their whites. *Courtesy of Lake of the Woods and Greenwoods Camps.*

Hanging out at Circle in 1982. *Left to right:* Mike Nekritz, Steve Adelman, Beth Jastromb, Abby Ripes, Robbie Munic, Dayna Glasson and an unidentified Greenwoods camper. *Courtesy of Lake of the Woods and Greenwoods Camps.*

days and, for the older kids, coed trips to the Warren Dunes and the Bryn Mawr/Mohawk Trip. And of course, there was Circle.

The poor kids spent all day watching the opposite sex run, laugh and play. The walk from the road to the waterfront was like a dusty runway for girls to strut their stuff for any hapless boy within distance. And in the Mess Hall, there were wonderful opportunities for the girls to be noticed or give a quick smile or giggle to their boyfriends when they walked through the boys' side to refill a plate of sloppy joes. And for the boys, it was always a treat. This was especially so during dinner, when the majority of Lake of the Woods had showered and put on clean clothes. Even from across the dining room, the entire camp of girls looked radiant. Ah…the scent of fruity and flowery shampoo with the aroma of apple crisp was the most powerful pheromone known—and it only existed at camp.

> *"We didn't bang the underside of the table and yell 'Schwing!' for nothing."*
> —*Doug Bates, camper/ counselor, 1985–2005*
>
> *"Many years after being a camper, I realized why you made us smack the bottom of the table when a pretty girl walked by. I didn't understand it when I was fourteen."*
> —*Dan Goldman, camper, 1996–2000*

In the Mess Hall, no relationship was a secret. No dirty laundry went unaired. Not with the "Knit One, Purl Two" at the ready. Before it was a chant at lunchtime, these were nothing more than knitting instructions. A knit stitch and a purl stitch are used to secure two different pieces of yarn. So it's obvious why the knitting term made its way to define young love at Lake of the Woods and Greenwoods. As soon as the mocking sound of a "Knit One, Purl Two" was sung about you, you were attached to the other named person regardless of truth to the contrary.

Knit one, purl two!
Jacob Simms, this is for you!
Where there's lipstick, you'll find makeup
Where there's Rebecca, YOU'LL FIND JACOB!

Granted, sometimes the songs were forced to have a slant rhyme, but the message was clear. Sometimes the "Knit Ones" would be like breaking news, and when the other person's name was dropped, each table in the Mess Hall collectively started asking, "Who did they say?" and, "They are?" or exclaiming, "That's not true!" Most of the "Knit Ones" were orchestrated and sung by the older cabins—the ones with the strongest hormones. They were not unlike animal mating calls across a thick forest. Navajo would sing one. Vassar would retaliate. Bryn Mawr would sing one. Mohawk would retaliate. Then Bryn Mawr would sing:

> *Bryn Mawr! Bryn Mawr! Bryn Mawr, Bryn Mawr, Bryn Mawr!*
> *We don't drink and we don't smoke and we don't go with Mohawk!*
> *Bryn Mawr! Bryn Mawr! Bryn Mawr, Bryn Mawr, Bryn Mawr!*

Mohawk responded:

> *Go back! Go back! Go back to the woods!*

The biggest challenge, however, wasn't coming up with a rhyme; it was getting the message out loud and clear. The Mess Hall was a noisy place with terrible acoustics. So the older cabins often enlisted other tables and even cabins as young as Iroquois or Hockaday to sing their songs. Although the younguns might not have understood the references or jumbled the words, the important part was getting the first two lines out: "Knit one, purl two! Mandy Rieff, this is for you!" Once those lines were heard, everyone instinctively became quiet to hear the rest of the song, which the older kids then delivered with ease. There was nothing more pathetic than a failed "Knit One, Purl Two."

They were much more than just songs about couples. They were a way to communicate. For example, Radcliffe cabin might have had a campfire scheduled with Comanche that night, and the cabin would sing:

> *Knit one, purl two!*
> *Comanche cabin, we like you!*

That would be it. It was like an early form of texting. Why write the entire word when two letters will suffice? Why sing the whole song when the sentiment is clear?

A Camp Story

"I was never worthy of a 'Knit One, Purl Two.' I wanted to cross that line just like Arrowhead and Color Days captain."

—Dan Goldwin

Once during my senior Mohawk year, without telling anyone else, I shouted at the top of my lungs, "Knit one, purl two!" and then shut up. The entire Mess Hall got quiet waiting for the rest of it. But there wasn't a rest of it. I just wanted to see if I could get the place quiet by myself. And I could. And that was a good day for me. This became a bad habit until I tried doing it just by shouting the word "Knit!" My acting out and, really, probably just more the annoyance of the whole thing cost me Circle that night. I never sang a "Knit One, Purl Two" alone again.

Before Circle was an option, you paid your dues as a younger camper at coed campfires. Often the idea for one of these campfires came from the camper with the most advanced set of hormones, and an invitation was sent out to the cabin of interest. This was done either by the counselors talking it over and setting it up like a parent would a play date or, in a more charming way, like through a "Knit One, Purl Two."

Sometimes the invited cabin was hotly contested among the bunkmates. Should there be more than one cabin with thirteen-year-olds, as was often the case, a choice had to be made between one and the other. The boys could've had girlfriends or interests in different cabins leading to the argument. And the girls were dealt the same conundrum. It was settled with a vote, or the counselors made the call based on an interest they had in a fellow counselor of one of the cabins across the road.

Occasionally, no decision had to be made at all. Campfires with coeds were held hostage from the kids, the ransom being good behavior or a high score in the day's cabin cleanup. If the agreed-on score was not met, the campfire was off. And on occasion, an invitation was turned down flat through embarrassing public rejection.

Knit one, purl two!
Cherokee cabin, this is for you!
Where there's a car, you'll find a tire
Where there's Briargate, YOU WON'T FIND A FIRE!

The History of Lake of the Woods and Greenwoods Camps

A campfire with the twelve- and thirteen-year-olds was like drops of oil dancing on a hot frying pan. The boys and girls scattered about the campfire circle in same-sex groups until one of the groups—usually the girls—approached a boy group. While the hormones mingled, the shyer kids sat quietly on the bench playing with sticks or a Rubix Cube or Game Boy. Eventually, one of the boys used a can of aerosol bug spray to ignite a small pyrotechnic show that made the girls shriek and run down the road toward the stables, while his cabin mates scolded him for wrecking their game. The counselor would wrangle her girls and herd them back to the campfire circle, while the boys' counselor confiscated the bug spray and made the perpetrator sit on the bench farthest removed from the activity.

A campfire with cabins any younger than that mostly resulted in boys staying on their side of the fire and girls on theirs. This gave the counselors a chance to do their own flirting or play matchmaker for their campers. This continued until one of the boys sprayed bug spray on the fire.

It's fair to say that boys never really grow up, and girls only pretend to not like the childish behavior. It's charming to mix fire with a concussive can of Deep Woods Off. And girls always have, and always will, like a bad boy. It's just not ladylike admitting to such taste. But at fourteen years old, immaturity is not something either side of the road will confess to. And that's because immature campers don't get to go to Circle.

Camp could be a dirty place, what with bug juice dripping through spiked cups onto your white camp logoed T-shirt or your shoes caked in six layers of mud after the tug-of-war battle. The lake was a perfectly clean lake, but it was no substitute for a hot shower and shampoo. If it weren't for Circle, there'd be no reason to ever get clean because you were just going to end up downwind of the campfire smoke and stink.

But there *was* Circle. And it was incredible. While most of the girls cleaned up before dinner, the boys waited until after evening program so as not to waste soap just to run around for two hours playing capture the flag. The girls had hair dryers, hair flatirons, hair curlers, hairspray, lipstick, eyeliner and perfumes. To see a group of young girls fuss over their looks was nothing out of the ordinary. The overwhelming odor of the combined chemicals that wafted out of their cabins was expected.

It was different with boys. Following evening program, Mohawks and, in later years, Blackhawks rushed like rats fleeing a sinking ship to the shower house. Mohawk Privilege was put into effect, which meant that any other camper had to give up his spot in line so a Mohawk could shower first. Sometimes boys were pulled right out of the shower so a Mohawk could catch some warm water. And if any of the younger boys talked back or protested, well, they might find themselves hanging from the Mohawk cabin grundie hook as retribution for their insolence.

The grundie hook was simple but feared. A "grundie" is another term for a wedgie. It's shorthand for undie grundie, when a kid's underwear is lifted out of his shorts by the waistband with the goal to floss the boy's posterior. I remain gender specific because I have never heard of girls giving one another wedgies. The grundie hook was a screw-hook in one of the support beams in Mohawk cabin. It was about three feet off the ground—the perfect height for an elastic waistband to support a sixty-pound Sioux camper while gravity did the work.

The only thing that trumped Mohawk Privilege was Counselor Privilege. Counselors were in a rush because they didn't want to miss their ride to town for their nights off. But no kids were ever pulled out of a stall. Counselor Privilege was far more civilized.

A promotional photo, circa early '60s. *Courtesy of Lake of the Woods and Greenwoods Camps.*

The History of Lake of the Woods and Greenwoods Camps

Once showered, the preening began back at the cabin. The care that went into getting their hair just right would be considered metrosexual today. Jeans and closed-toed shoes, with tucked-in T-shirts or buttoned-down oxfords or flannel shirts. Really, anything that was just slightly nicer than what was worn between the Ski Dock and the Riflery Range. Many of these clothes were hung in the closet on reserve and dubbed "Circle clothes." This dress was the norm for most Mohawks, except for Edmundo del Valle, a camper and counselor throughout the 1990s from Mexico City. He always dressed like he had just stepped out of a fashion ad in *Quién* magazine.

> *"The first night of Circle my senior Bryn year was like an entirely new beginning—like absolutely anything was possible, and I remember having the sense that everyone else thought that same thing. It was a moment when everyone let go of any cliques—even if they'd been the same cliques for five years. It was just a night of hope. It was the one night I can remember that was drama-free."*
> *—Lauren Cohn, camper/counselor, 1990–99*

It was typical coed teenage interaction. The boys teased the girls, and they said they hated it but really loved every minute of the attention. Inside jokes were made that would later lead to sketches in the Bryn Mawr Show. Couples paired off and sat on one of the white benches holding hands or snuck off behind the Girls' Rec Lodge to do a little necking on the silo base. A daring couple might try to go into the rec lodge to get some time on the large red gymnastics mat being stored for the night. Should a counselor catch anyone not in the Circle area, they were quickly rounded up and moved back to be with the rest of the horn dogs.

Doug Bates and Kim Simmons in 1993. *Courtesy of David Himmel.*

> *"Growing up, Circle is what you looked forward to doing as a senior camper. If you were lucky to have a camp girlfriend you would try and sit in the dark, away from the others and hold hands or sneak a kiss. Maybe share some Gummi Bears from Canteen."*
> —Doug Bates

Mostly, Circle was an hour of boiling-hot hormones and empty drama fueled by the oversensitive feelings driven by puberty and ego. It ended either in a clear victory or defeat. At 10:00 p.m., the Mohawks crossed the road back to the cabin, and Bryn Mawrs giggled along the cabin path back to theirs. A good night was when you talked to the boy or girl you liked. A bad night was one of loneliness that left you forlorn.

Because the majority of camp life was restricted to camp property, there was no real way for couples to go out on a date. Sure, there were dances, but that was like a group date with little siblings around to bug you.

Therefore, the Bryn Mawr/Mohawk Trip was the Super Bowl of Circle. All session, you laid the groundwork for a relationship to be something considered adult and real. And so, at the end of the session, you could have an actual, all-expenses-paid date with your sweetie…and the rest of your friends. A night on the town! A night in Portage, Michigan.

> *"It used to be the biggest deal ever, like who was going to sit on the bus with Justin Lawrence."*
> —Dana Cohn, camper/counselor/girls' program director/associate director, 1991–present

It was date night at camp, and everyone had to look his or her best. The Bryn Mawr/Mohawk Trip followed the classic date formula of dinner and a movie. Discussion began over what restaurant to eat at several days before. Movies were made available by rating and time. In the early '90s, the restaurant debate became moot when prior years showed that the consensus was to have Chinese food. Panda Forest is now strict tradition, followed by a film at the Crossroads Mall movieplex.

Bryn Mawrs and Mohawks heading out for the Bryn Mawr/Mohawk Trip. *Courtesy of Eric Himmel.*

A trip to the outside world, where cups were made of glass and there were no Xs on the corners of the tables, gave cause to feel both out of place and like something special. It was an opportunity to show the opposite sex what you were like during colder months. The movie made for a chance to see the summer blockbuster and return to the suburbs at the end of the season without feeling like you missed out on too much. But above all, it was a chance for teenagers to hang out in the real world for a night.

For many of these teenagers, it was Circle that first presented them with the flirtatious ritual in such an intimate setting—under starry nights with the smell of Canteen popcorn and bug spray in the air. Josh Troy, a Mohawk in 1992 and '93, was one such teenager.

"I was just starting to really interact with the opposite sex. I was impressionable and wanted to be cool. Well, as a huge sitcom fan, I tried to be cool by taking after The Fonz from *Happy Days*. I tried to pick up girls by snapping my fingers just like The Fonz did," Josh said. "I remember my peers being amused by this because I actually thought it would win me a date. It did not work…It did, however, get me talking to girls and making friends with them for the first time. If nothing else, I learned what *not* to do."

Things aren't like that today. Circle was held in the actual circle of white benches in front of the Big House under the night sky. Now, Circle is in the

Miller Pavilion under fluorescents. The busses for the trip to Portage aren't even coed. It's hardly a date night anymore. It's a chance to put on some decent threads and get out of camp for a few hours. And maybe that's a good thing. Think of the broken hearts gender-specific busses are preventing.

Sometimes the route to love is an embarrassing one, and a summer at Lake of the Woods and Greenwoods offered plenty of moments to crash and burn or to reach the nirvana of cool. Dances, and the days leading up to them, were like hormone hunting season.

Each session hosted two dances. One was held on any regular night as evening program. Today, these first dances are called Halloween Dances, where campers and counselors dress up as cabin groups in bizarre and entertaining costumes. The other dances coincided with a coed special day like International Day or the Fourth of July's Carnival Day. Dances were held in Louis Lodge and, as the camp grew, the Boys' Rec Lodge, until they were moved to the Pavilion between the Big House and the Girls' Rec Lodge.

Music was provided by whatever records, tapes, CDs and, eventually, mp3s that campers and counselors brought with them. Quite often, one or two Mohawks deejayed the dance from the stage. Music was gathered during the day or a few days before if a mixed tape was needed.

In the early 1990s, under the assistant directorship of Dayna, Chicago-based deejay dance companies were hired. There was always a burst of excitement and nerves when the deejay company started its sound test and bass reverberated throughout the camp. This was an incredibly sweet gig for the company because although it was a four-hour round-trip drive from Chicago to play a two-hour party, it was the best advertising a company could ask for. Consider a room full of preened, young, mostly Jewish kids preparing for their bar and bat mitzvahs, each one silently shopping for the next big party idea. For the company, it was like shooting gefilte fish in a barrel.

The days and hours leading up to the dance were wrought with hype and bursts of anxiety about whom to take or whom to ask to dance when the slow songs played. What to wear was never an issue because everyone packed specific dance outfits reserved for the occasions. In 1991, I fancied white denim shorts. And when I spilled orange bug juice on them at dinner just before the dance, I nearly came unglued.

On those coed special days, the dance was a part of Sadie Hawkins Day, an American tradition that's been around since its debut in 1937 in the *Li'l Abner* comic strip. Sadie was a character known as the "homeliest gal in the hills." Her father initiated the idea for the women of the town to chase the bachelors rather than wait to be wooed. He did this mostly because he didn't want Sadie living at home with him. Almost immediately, the idea took off, and high schools and college campuses were hosting their own Sadie Hawkins Days. The end result in the comic strip was marriage. Such was the case at camp.

Following rest hour, the girls made their way to the Boys' Sports Field and lined up at the road closest to Timber Trails. The boys wore socks in their waistbands, just the same as one would during a game of capture the flag. They gathered across the field at the tree line. A counselor acted as officiator and sounded the bullhorn alarm to start the hunt.

The girls took off like bats out of hell, and the boys scattered. It was a melee of love, a busy hive of sweaty hormones swarming all about. Madness. Some boys surrendered to their girls. Others made them work for that sock, running fast, ducking and dodging. Sometimes girls enlisted their friends to flank the boy they wanted. Some weren't chased at all. Some didn't want to chase.

After a few minutes, the counselor/officiator sounded the alarm again, ending the hunt. Those nabbed lined up with their captors and were given small, bronze-colored foil rings. The officiator said a few words like:

Today we gather…hot and sweaty after running around a sports field in ninety-degree heat…to witness the pure sanctity of marriage between all of these lovely couples…some of which probably need their parents' permission to get married, but we'll worry about that later…now, before we all rehydrate, do you boy, who got caught by the girl looking at you, take her to be your wife for the rest of the day until the dance is over, to be honest and kind and dance with her at least once…and girl who caught the boy…are you cool with all that…please place your toy rings on one another's finger…I now pronounce you husband and wife…nobody kiss…this is not a coed camp.

"It's probably the best and worst part of Fourth of July," said Lauren Yanow, a camper, counselor-in-training and junior counselor between 1999 and 2006. Lauren's Briargate year was the first she had a camp boyfriend. Their relationship, like most of the campers' relationships, revolved around meeting at Circle after lunch.

"I never cared about the Sadie Hawkins dance before," she said. "But now that I had a boyfriend, everything was different. Boys are much faster than girls, so this tends to be a very embarrassing event—especially for someone as un-athletic as myself. I was so nervous. What if someone got to him before I did? What if he ran away from me?"

At the start, he did run away from her. See, you have to understand something about boys. Sadie Hawkins Day is one of only a few times in a young boy's life when he can make the girls really work for his affections. Males of all ages rarely get the chance to play hard-to-get. Many of us are stuck playing hard-to-want. Sadie Hawkins is a nice break from the norm, so this kid took advantage of it. Eventually, he slowed down. Lauren got her man, and they were hitched.

The dance was a few hours later. As usual, a good majority of Lake of the Woods showered and dressed before dinner. The problem with getting cleaned up for a Sadie Hawkins dance before dinner is that there was always the outdoor barbecue. And that meant delicious but messy sauce-smothered chicken and ribs. One was wise to wait until after dinner to get gussied up. Remember my lesson learned in 1991.

"I put on one of the two preplanned outfits I brought with me for these events and went off to the dance," Lauren said.

Across the road, the green shingles of the Boys' Rec Lodge were shaking from the thrum of the music. The cabin area reeked of cologne and deodorant. Greenwoods campers begged their counselors for a spray or roll of Right Guard and a spritz or a splash of Drakkar Noir. It was nights like these when boys learned that a little cologne goes a long way but a lot will get you nowhere. Mohawks unnecessarily shaved in preparation for that cheek-to-cheek slow dance.

Kessler never had to worry about this. It's not that he didn't have to shave—in fact, his body was dense in light-blond hair—it's that Kessler never had a cheek-to-cheek dance. A camper from 1990 to 1993, he had a terrible case of asthma, which required him to take several medications, including prednisone, a corticosteroid that stunted his growth. He may have been shorter than most everyone in camp, including some Iroquois campers, but Kessler had an advantage the rest of us did not. Not only was he one of the most well-liked people at camp, and a systematically charming ladies' man, but Kessler was also the exact right height so that when he danced with a Bryn Mawr or Vassar, his head rested just so on her chest. "Envy" is the only word that came to mind. I suppose "honorable" and "awesome" would be good words to describe it, too.

He went off the major meds later and zoomed straight up like a rocket in height. He's still the smooth-operating Casanova making a living as the director of customer development at the Artisan Hotel Boutique in Las Vegas. But not everyone was as comfortable as Kessler at making moves at the dances.

The History of Lake of the Woods and Greenwoods Camps

Crammed in the rec lodge, music blaring, everyone sweating, the pungent odor of a cologne factory explosion in the air, Lauren—even though she ran her butt off and got married to her man—was playing coy.

"Eventually I went and found my husband, and we slow-danced to all my favorite songs," she said. For those who did not want to dance, a movie was always shown across the road in the Girls' Rec Lodge. This would have provided a perfect time and place for a make-out session, but it was still light out, and the counselor assigned to the movie was on the watch for puckered lips and wandering hands.

When the sun did go down and the dance ended, it was like herding cats getting the boys and girls to their cabins. Kids huddled around the ping-pong tables to scarf down cookies and juice with hopes of squeezing a little more magic out of the night. But on the Fourth of July, the village of Decatur hosted a fireworks show visible from the waterfront. And the entire camp gathered along the shoreline to "Ooh" and "Ahh" at the popping and booming.

"Since it was 'not a coed camp,' we were supposed to spend the fireworks with our cabins," said Lauren. "I said goodbye to my boyfriend and went with my friends to find a spot by the lake. Just as the fireworks were starting, I felt someone tap my shoulder. My boyfriend snuck away from his cabin. I quietly snuck away, too, and we went to a different spot to watch. After a few minutes of holding hands and watching the fireworks above, we had to go back to our cabins so we wouldn't get caught."

It seemed that there was never enough time spent with the person you liked. So we did what we had to do to get more time. We snuck out.

A successful sneak-out required patience, cunning and black clothes. If anyone was brave enough to sneak into a cabin for a squeaky-bunk make-out session, there was only one tried-and-true route from cabin area to cabin area. Coming from the boys' side, it was best to slither along the cabin lines, using every structure shadow as cover. Once you made it to the bush at the corner of Mohawk cabin, you could rest and take a long, hard look at the Boys' Sports Field, the road and the Archery Range to be certain that no one was around.

This stretch was the most dangerous because you were completely exposed. One by one, you'd make a mad dash from the cabin area, across the road, under the Archery Range rope, through the range and into the woods along the path leading to the tennis courts.

From there, you had the protection of trees but had to walk softly to not rustle branches, rocks or leaves. The next obstacle was crossing from the woods, under the parking lot light, to either the courts and to the small bit of broken fence that could be peeled back (it was this way for decades) or straight across the parking lot to the road and into the trees and bushes that separated the girls' camp from $47^{th}1/2$ Street. You'd walk along the foliage until you were perpendicular to the desired cabin and then dart across the cabin area to meet your girls.

If the girls ever came to the boys' cabins, they could take the same route in reverse. In 1994, our respective girlfriends visited Jacob Simms, Justin Lawrence and me in our Mohawk cabin. We thought we were done for when Program Director Troy Broussard and Quiz stormed in because they claimed that they heard girls and saw shadowy figures lurking around the cabin. Our girls dove under our beds fast. Jacob, Justin and I pretended to sleep.

"Check his breathing, Quiz," Troy said in a whisper. "See if his heartbeat's racing." Troy was a United States Army vet. His past was a little mysterious, and we were all certain he was going to find us out. While Troy stood by our three beds and lazily looked around, Quiz put his head on my chest and his finger under my nose.

"Davey's fine," he said. "Sound asleep." Of course I wasn't, but I did everything I could to keep myself calm—slow my heartbeat, ease my breathing. He checked Justin with the same results.

"I'll check Jacob," Troy said. I assume he ran the same diagnostics on Jacob as Quiz had on Justin and me, but Jacob was not as lucky. "Simms is awake," Troy said. "Come on, Jacob, get up. We know you're awake."

I heard Jacob sit up and shout, "I'm not awake! I'm sleeping. Let me sleep!" He woke the rest of the cabin, including our counselors, at which point Troy and Quiz laughed maniacally and ran out.

None of us ever spoke about what happened that night. We were guilty of having girls over, the girls were guilty of being over and I'm sure Troy and Quiz were guilty of being hung-over the next day. Had it been a legit cabin check, they would have looked under the beds. So we all acted like it never went down.

If you were going to meet up with a girl or boy, it was always best to wait until after the ODs were finished for the night, so anytime after 1:00 a.m. would suffice. You did have to be careful of the night watchman, other counselors sneaking out for a rendezvous or waking up your own counselor before you even left the cabin. And it was always best to meet anywhere but in the cabin. The Riflery Range, the teepee, Campcraft and the Go-Cart Track were all prime spots.

The History of Lake of the Woods and Greenwoods Camps

> *"We tried to sneak over to the boys' side but never made it. The counselors always caught us."*
>
> *—Linda Baskind Rosenberg*

Sneaking out was never encouraged at either camp. Lauren Cohn was found in a Greenwoods cabin in 1993. Marc called her parents in Hyde Park to report the dangerous stunt she pulled by sneaking out unsupervised at night. Her father's response was, "That's my girl!" Some kids were sent home. After the Troy and Quiz raid on our cabin in 1994, Jacob's girlfriend, Rebecca Kaplan, did finally get busted and was shipped back to the 'burbs.

If a kid gets caught sneaking out today, parents don't cheer them; they put the fault on the counselors and the camp and its directors, but certainly not the sneaky camper. The first strike, it's a call home. The second strike, it's the Rebecca Kaplan Highway for you. The camp is as strict as it's ever been about sneaking out. So if kids are going to do it, it better be for love. But let the record show that I do not condone this behavior.

Lake of the Woods and Greenwoods Camps are officially called brother and sister camps. But they are more than that. They are, at times, the best of friends, the greatest of enemies and the kindest of lovers. The two camps need each other because camp is more than playing jacks and grundie hooks. It's finding out who you are. And kids would have never known who they were if there weren't those strange and funny creatures across the road to help them find out.

Chapter 8

CAMPERS, COUNSELORS, BEST OF ALL

There was no rent, they were going to feed me and pay me a salary of $1,200.
—"Big" James Boulware

John "Windo" Windomaker is a legend. Just say his name to anyone who was at Lake of the Woods or Greenwoods in the 1980s and early 1990s, and the way their eyes widen you know they're about to rattle off a wild Windo story. Here he tells one of his own:

> *Here's the gig. I saw an ad in the newspaper. It said, "We're looking for counselors." I just graduated from high school, and I needed a job. I called and they said, "How old are you?" I told them I was eighteen. "Sorry, you have to be nineteen."*
>
> *I went to my dad and told him what happened. And Dad said, "Lie. That's what kids do. Call back and lie to get the job." So I did. I told them I was nineteen. I was qualified because I taught swimming lessons at the YMCA for years, and I landed a job at the Swim Dock.*
>
> *Jeff Miner was the first person I met at camp. It was 1984. We were standing by the Boys' Sports Field, and he was throwing a fricking boomerang. I said, "Hi, my name is John." He said, "My name is Jeff. I'm throwing a boomerang, think you can catch it?" He said he was an English major and I thought, "What the hell have I done?"*

Left to right: Jeff "the Magic Counselor" Miner and John "Windo" Windomaker in 1987. *Courtesy of Jeff Miner.*

Windo worked at camp three summers before Marc realized that his birthday was *December* 17, 1965, and not *February* 17, 1965. By that time, Windo was old enough and valued enough as a counselor that the little white lie he had told about his age three years earlier didn't matter. He was also well into solidifying his reputation with the campers and the rest of the staff.

"I made friends with the ski instructors and found out I was pretty good at [skiing], so I eventually moved there," he said. One of those instructors was Tom Longo, known as the Bronze God. Longo was from Nebraska and incredibly quiet. He never seemed to fit in but was entirely comfortable at camp. When he laughed, it was boisterous. "You always felt in some way that he was protecting Windo," Dan said. "Because Windo was a loose cannon, but he was always great to campers."

"When I first got there, because I was so young, Seeger called me Peachfuzz, and he decided I'd be best with the little kids in Iroquois," Windo said. "I had this one kid who crapped his pants every day. Now, I came from a respectable, lower-middle-class family where that was unacceptable. But I was dealing with kids from Chicago's North Shore, and management told me to deal with it and keep his privacy."

"Then it got better," he continued. "I was in Sioux, Chippewa…my favorite cabin was Navajo. There were three counselors in that cabin: me, Todd Lough and Brad Clark. We had some serious fun. We would sneak the kids out way back behind where the Climbing Wall is now and light off bottle rockets I brought from home."

The rule against fireworks at camp withstanding, it *was* a cabin activity and adults *were* supervising the kids. Windo had a sense for what boys needed—adventure, danger, excitement, risk…and guidance. "I kept going back to try and teach them," he said.

The relationship between counselors and campers could make or break a summer. "Sol Ashbach was the coolest kid I ever knew," Windo said. "He talked to me like he was my age. He had it going on. I had this one kid, Benjy Litwin, he was my [counselor-in-training] in Cherokee in '88. I'll never forget what he said to me. He was a killer at cabin cleanup, I never really cared about it, but he did and I asked him about it one time, you know, why he cared so much. He told me his *maid* taught him. Yeah, he cleaned it up well."

Benjy was also a Red Team captain in 1986, with his counselor pal Windo as Red Team advisor. Marc knew Windo was a leader, a role model even,

Evening program at Greenwoods: campers versus counselors pillow fight. *Courtesy of David Himmel.*

and he built incredible relationships with his campers. "He took great care of my little brother Bobby and me," Dan said. "One summer, he even drove me home because my parents were on vacation and couldn't pick me up."

At times, though, Windo and Marc clashed. "Rainy day? My response was, let's everyone take our shoes off and go play soccer. So what if it was fifteen or thirty guys on each side, let's play. Marc was afraid someone would get hurt. I remember that if I felt like playing baseball, I would get on the microphone in the program cabin and call the kids out to play baseball. And we'd play."

Windo calls it rebellion. But it was always for the enjoyment of everyone else and added to the camp experience. Clashes and all, it was clear that "Seeger loved him like a son," Dan said.

Getting into trouble with the counselors was part of bonding—pushing the limits, trying new things and growing up together. This is why kitchen raids were so much fun to go on with counselors. Raids were sanctioned by the program director so the cabin could be empty without the ODs flipping out. Also, this made sure there was enough ice cream or cookies to be raided in the Mess Hall. But a good counselor wouldn't tell this to the kids. The cabin members remained under the impression that they were about to break some serious rules and risked getting kicked out and their counselor even getting fired. Occasionally, counselors had other counselors pretend to catch the cabin, which caused the campers' hearts to race and their adrenaline to boil over and let them experience an even greater level of fun once they ran off and dove into the woods for cover.

Sometimes the lies were at the campers' expense. In 1993, Troy and Mohawk counselor Andrew "Shaggy" Cannon wanted to have a little fun with a Mohawk named Jeff "Big Bird" Feldman. Jeff was a well-liked kid. But he was goofy. He earned the nickname Big Bird because he was tall with a head full of bright-blond hair that made his appearance resemble the famed *Sesame Street* character.

Jeff never snuck out, but he wanted to, and he pressed his friends in the cabin to sneak out with him one night. So they did. But not before telling Shaggy about it, who in turn told Troy. And a plan was devised to teach Jeff the lesson that sneaking out of the cabin was a terribly dangerous thing to do.

Late, about the time just after the ODs signed off, Aaron Finkelstein, Brad Gordon, Jonathan Rosenberg, Rory Zacher and Jeff slinked out of their beds. Dressed head to toe in black, they quietly moved out of the cabin, holding the spring of the door to silence the squeak. The boys

Left to right: boys' program director Troy Broussard and Mohawk counselor Andrew "Shaggy" Cannon. *Photo by David Himmel.*

didn't make it far before Troy and Shaggy caught them on the Archery Range. Everyone acted shocked and worried, but Jeff was legitimately concerned. Troy and Shaggy were talking about sending them home for the summer.

Then Shaggy, the funniest and most laidback counselor in Greenwoods history, came unhinged. He paced and kicked dirt, stomped the ground and scolded the boys more and more violently. Each bark was less and less like the Shaggy these boys knew. Troy tried to calm him down, but that aggravated whatever beast was controlling him. After a few minutes of Shaggy's manic hollering, Troy looked at Jeff and screamed, "Run, Jeff, run! Shaggy's lost it!"

Jeff may not have run that fast in his life or since. He sprinted straight across the Archery Range, his long, thin legs a blur in the pale light, and in a moment, his bright-blond hair disappeared into the woods.

Shaggy, Troy and the boys waited to see if he'd return. After a minute or so, they all burst into hysterical laughter. Once they composed themselves, they went to find Jeff. Following a quick sweep of the woods, the Mohawks were sent back to their cabin. It took Shaggy and Troy another hour before they found him. He had made his way into the thickest part of the woods between the stables and the Archery Field and shimmied up a tree, where he hid, frightened for his friends and his rabid counselor.

Jeff had every right to be upset about the prank. But when he returned to the cabin with Shaggy and Troy, he was laughing with them, happy to have been part of the fun.

Dealing with kids freaking out isn't always a laugh riot. Marc had a colossal hatred of vomit. Couldn't stand to see it, smell it, hear it coming up or talk about it. In the middle of the night, when Marc was a counselor in Chippewa, a camper woke him up to tell him he was sick. Marc walked the kid to the bathroom and stayed there with the boy while he puked his guts up.

When it stopped, Marc thought he was in the clear until the boy cried out, "My retainer!"

"What about your retainer?"

"It came out when I threw up."

"Well, where is it?" The kid said nothing.

"It's in the toilet?"

"Yes."

"Why didn't you take it out of your mouth first!" The boy was too sick and distraught to take action on his own, and Marc couldn't let a camper's retainer get flushed away—retainers have a street value of hundreds of dollars. So, Marc reached into the toilet bowl of fresh vomit to fish out the boy's retainer. He went deep, to the very bottom, and swirled his hand and forearm around as he searched for the plastic and metal restraint. Eventually, he pulled it from the bile—sometimes counselors will do anything for their campers.

Lifelong friendships can be forged between counselors and their campers. During the Greenberg era, the camp always celebrated Mrs. G.'s birthday on August 4. Every camper allotted Canteen money to buy Mrs. G. a gift. Quite often, they were rather fine gifts such as Steuben glassware. Many of Mrs. G.'s campers and counselors remained close throughout the rest of her life. "There was a group of us that was invited whenever she had a birthday celebration," said Roselle. On her eightieth birthday in 1977, Mrs. G. had a party at the Highland Park Country Club, and many camp friends attended. "She threw me an engagement shower in her apartment on Lake Shore Drive."

I was fortunate enough to have been a counselor in a cabin with the same kids two years in a row. They were good kids—screwy, funny and loads of fun. And they were sweet, very concerned for my well-being. In 1997, we were in Chippewa cabin. The boys knew the rule during rest hour was that they didn't have to nap or stay on their own beds but that they had to be on someone's bed, talking or playing quietly. Like I said, these were good kids, so I trusted them not to hurt themselves or burn the place down while I grabbed a quick nap.

On this particular day, when the announcement for third period came, I woke up covered in shattered glass. Still groggy from the nap, I looked around at all of the boys in their personal areas, quietly and carefully getting ready for their next activity. "Guys?" I said. I looked up and saw that the window above my bed was broken. "Why am I covered in glass? What happened to my window?"

The funniest of the kids and easily one of my favorite campers, "Psycho Mike" Mikey Goldberg, came forward, his tail between his legs. "We were throwing a golf ball around and it went through your window."

"What's the matter with you?"

"We didn't mean to break anything."

"Obviously. Why didn't you wake me up?" I was also kind of surprised that the sound of shattering glass just above my head hadn't woken me up, but rest hour naps were deep naps. No one responded. Mikey just looked at me, his eleven-year-old cherub face riddled with guilt. "Why didn't you wake me up?" I asked again.

"We didn't want to. We know you need your rest."

I had to laugh. I mean, I was angry with them for breaking the rules and putting themselves in harm's way, but I had to consider their selective thoughtfulness. "Next time you do something stupid while I'm asleep, wake me up. And you all lose Canteen tomorrow." They apologized and the following day scored a 98 in cabin cleanup. They also knew how much I liked a clean cabin.

Perhaps the greatest hoax the staff ever pulled on the campers was Outer Space Day, a coed special day in 1969. "The day itself was real," said Linda. "But I don't remember one thing about it. But the lead up to it, the night before…the kids were terrified." Following is a combined remembrance from Linda and Shelly:

> *We planned it starting the first week of camp. We all knew our roles. During evening program, the Decatur police came roaring into Circle, and Laurie comes out to talk to them. Then he called Dan and Lorraine to the Circle. Lorraine was a tough lady, everyone knew that, but she broke down and started crying.*
>
> *She told us to go back to our cabins and then came around to tell all of us that there had been a UFO sighting and that it could land at camp. I was in the Hockaday cabin, and several of them were crying.*
>
> *We told them, "No radios. Just stay put. We're going to have to evacuate camp." Counselors who didn't smoke were smoking, trying to act more nervous. When it got dark, we all were told to go to the Mess Hall. The guys built this frame, this large circle out of wood…*
>
> *It was covered with sails from the sailboats, and there were old car lights underneath it flashing.*
>
> *Then this creature—the big maintenance guy, Mike, all dressed up—came out…The kids were freaking out. All of the kids were crying and throwing up everywhere. The creature made an announcement…*

The History of Lake of the Woods and Greenwoods Camps

"Welcome Camp Greenwoods and Lake of the Woods. We are Martians and this is to announce our special Outer Space Day…We are going to test you earthlings by splitting you up into two teams." Then we had the stupid special day. I couldn't tell you one activity that we did. But kids were throwing up. They were pissed.

Outer Space Day never happened again.

Camp counselors are the perfect blend of authority figure and friend. "You think about your life," said Shelly, now an attorney in Chicago.

I'm a great believer that every kid should have one to three adults outside of the family—someone who is not obligated to be their friend and support them—to be a mentor, a role model. I try to be that for younger lawyers. In my life, there have been several. But there is none more important than Dan Langell.

A thoughtful and heartfelt letter from Program Director Dan Langell in the 1964 camp yearbook. *Courtesy of Lake of the Woods and Greenwoods Camps.*

```
                                    Camp Greenwoods
                                    Decatur, Michigan
                                    August 20,1964

Dear Campers,

        As I write this Color Days are going strong.  Which
team will win I have no idea.  I hear Joey outside the
program cabin telling all who will agree that the teams
are now even according to his scoring.  I wonder if
he's right?

        It's a warm day with a few lazy clouds and the
temperature is in the 80's .  I imagine the weather
is a bit different while you are reading this.

        In spite of our weather board ( or maybe because
of it)  the weather this summer has been a bit extreme.
Extreme heat, extreme cold, extreme dry but boy when
it rained it really came down.  Remember visitor's day
when the heat hit 100 and the next week we were shivering
the morning the thermometer read 40.

        The weather may have been extreme but so was your
spirit.  A camp is only as good as the spirit of its
campers and b y this standard this summer was a fine
one.  Thanks to you, this was a great camping season.

        I don't want to stop without a word of appreciation
to the staff who worked so hard to help you have a good
summer.  I feel especially in debt to Dave Solomon who
was my assistant this year.  I've worked 5 years now
with Dave and he makes a good right hand.

        So we come to the end of another camping season
and the campfire will burn down into glowing embers
for the last time.  But next summer we'll meet again
and again kindle a campfire on the ashes of this
years last and the campfire will glow again in
truth as well as in our dreams.

        So long for now.  See you next year......

                        Dan Langell
```

111

*Dan kind of figured out that I was a thinker, and he started talking
to me about how things worked. I still use what he taught me when I'm
practicing law today. Every kid in camp had a relationship with Dan. If
you couldn't take it to your counselor, you could take it to Dan.*

Once you're a counselor in a cabin of kids, you'll always be concerned and
want the best for them. José Miguel Migoya was a camper turned counselor
between 1995 and 2005. "I liked being a counselor," he said. "It's good to see
you can make a change in one kid's life and that you can make them smile. I
look at two campers of mine on Facebook. One is in the Special Forces and
the other is a cop. They don't need me looking after them. They'll save *me*
one day. But I still worry and want to look out for them."

When Shelly was a counselor in 1967, he had a camper in his cabin with
a glass eye.

*He was this skinny kid, Johnny was his name…he was great in the water
but pretty bad at the sports on land. And we're playing baseball. Johnny's
at the plate, he's batting away. There was a counselor named Marty
Goldman, sarcastic, funny as hell. He was pitching, and he said to Johnny,
"Keep your eye on the ball." No one was sure if he said it to be funny or if
it just slipped out, but Johnny was a good sport about it.*

*The kids all liked him. They loved seeing him take his eye out then
pop it back in. But there was this one kid in the cabin who would tease
him about it. And I jumped all over that kid. It was the summer of the
"Six-Day War," and I said, "Tomorrow, I'll invite Moshe Dayan to come
over, would you like that?" That put a stop to the teasing real quickly.*
[Moshe Dayan, of course, was the one-eyed Israeli minister of
defense—a real badass.]

> *"If my father ever dies at sea, I will call Jeff Miner and ask him
> to be my father. I love that man."*
> —*Pablo Dragon Migoya, camper/counselor 1995–2002*

Windo scoffed when I referred to him as a legend. But counselors can
become sort of celebrities. In 1990, Dan was the head of the Sail Dock.
There was a group of eleven- and twelve-year-old girls who referred to him

Sailing instructor Dan Goldwin at the helm of the legendary *Putt-Putt* rescue dinghy. *Courtesy of Dan Bates.*

as Mr. President whenever they saw him. "I wanted to be the first Jewish president," he said. "They started saying, 'Sup, Mr. President.'" Later that summer, a new Sunfish sailboat was purchased. The campers voted to name it *Danny Boy*. Dan was the first staff member out of three to have a boat adorned with his name. The second was Lola. In 2002, Emily "Ferdie" Ferdman, a camper, counselor and full-time staffer from 1992 (and still today), had the SS *Ferdster* named in her honor.

In a moment found in the *This American Life* episode "Notes on Camp," three Vassar girls—Jamie Meisel, Mandi Miller and Carly Torch— approached me and show host Ira Glass as he interviewed me during one of the dances in 1998. They regaled him with unsolicited stories of why I was their favorite counselor. Then they sang a song they had written about me for him. The experience and the relationship with those girls was, and remains, humbling. I'm still flattered.

Today, when DC is walking the grounds, she is regularly greeted with hugs and high-fives and screeches from Lake of the Woods campers. The boys try to play it cool because she's pretty. But to these kids, DC is a goddess. She is an approachable celebrity. Tangible and someone they can really look up to. And why shouldn't they?

The majority of Lake of the Woods and Greenwoods campers always hailed from Chicagoland. During the Greenberg era, there was a strong Canadian contingency, and in the 1940s, a big group of girls from St. Louis came to camp. In fact, there was an entire cabin of *only* St. Louis girls. But demographics changed, and fifty years later, there were only two girls at camp from St. Louis, Kelly Bry and Lori Wolfson. Until the 1980s, most of the Chicago-based campers lived in South Shore or in the south suburbs versus places up north like Highland Park and Glencoe.

I grew up in Flossmoor, and I loved that for years I was the only kid from the south suburbs. Camp really was a completely different world for me. My camp friends who lived in Northbrook over the winter, well, they might as well have lived on the moon. Canada wasn't as strongly represented during Seegerville, but instead, our southern neighbor began sending its kids to camp.

"My family has always been concerned about how to get ahead in the world, so they wanted us to have the best experiences," José said. "They thought camp would be a great way to improve my English and build my self-confidence. I think I cried every day the first year. And then I cried when I said goodbye."

José, his brother, Pablo, and sister, Isabella, are from Mexico City. They were part of a large wave of Mexican campers and counselors that came to camp during Seegerville. "A lot of these kids went to camp and didn't talk to anyone but other Mexicans," he said. "And they ended up hating camp because they never got into the camp spirit. Pablo, Isabella and I, we made friends with Americans because that's what we were there to do…I learned a lot about the different cultures. I know how to get along with people from different countries, and that helps with business now and helps me with my job." José is a product brand manager for an international consumer product goods company. And that's quite a ways off from teaching tennis and soccer at camp. He wasn't even that good at soccer. But due to Mexico's culture—and truly, every other country in the world but the United States and Canada—soccer was a major sport that everyone played. So, as a Mexican, he was better than everyone else at camp. That is, except for the kitchen staff, which was made up of mostly eastern Europeans.

The geography of counselors also changed over the years. Laurie started hiring foreign staff in the late 1960s. At first, it was only the maintenance and kitchen positions because, he said, "American kids didn't want to work those jobs." Then it got harder to find enough qualified or certified domestic counselors for the activities because of availability. Universities and colleges started manipulating course schedules, and classes were starting earlier in the summer. Too many American college kids had to be back on campus in early August.

Camp America was formed in 1969 to offer "summer work adventures" to twentysomething Brits looking to travel abroad and make a little money along the way. When Camp Counselors USA was opened in 1985, it worked with young travelers from sixty other countries. Both Camp America and Camp Counselors USA handle details like visas, flights and most of the red tape that comes with working with foreigners.

"I had very few reference points to build an opinion of what I might be going to experience," said Guy Chatfield. "I came to camp out of curiosity, basically. The idea came from a friend who completed a summer at a U.S. camp as a dance teacher and counselor, and she enjoyed herself, so I thought I would give it a try."

Guy is from Scotland. He was a Greenwoods counselor and sailing instructor for two years, in 1992 and 1995. "This form of camping did not really happen in the UK in the early 1990s," he said.

> There are commercial operations that run loosely similar in style residential camps, which I attended as a child, but the concept is not even close to the popularity in the U.S.
>
> Where I came from, the loud culture, and its seemingly constant positive reinforcement, felt a bit weird at first—we Scots are a bit more reserved. And many of the campers were returning year after year, so they knew the place, the customs and other campers a million times better than I. This made me think some of the superconfident kids I met initially were brash, American brats.
>
> The sarcastic, dry British sense of humor was lost on lots of the Americans. The counselors from Australia and New Zealand shared this humor with me, and at times we were definitely laughing at people rather than with them. In retrospect, this was pretty mean.
>
> It wasn't long before I realized we were all very similar people deep down, with similar values and the desire to do well.

As much fun as it was being a counselor and hanging out with, teaching and laughing with the kids, there was an incredible joy received by spending time with the rest of the staff. "During the day, you get to play soccer and tennis with the kids and kind of be a kid yourself," said José. "Then at night, you can go and have a beer with your friends."

In town, there were two bars that were invaded with young, clean-cut counselors looking to tie one on. There was the Penny Lane Pub, a dance club that eventually closed and reopened as a strip joint called Scooters. "Everyone wanted to hang out at the Penny Lane," Windo said. "But I wanted to hang out at the local watering hole." That watering hole was the M-40. It had a pool table, a jukebox stacked with Top 40, country and oldies, cheap pitchers of beer and the creepiest stuffed raccoon in the world near the front booth. Because camp operated on a different time zone than Decatur, the bartenders kept the place open an hour later so the staff could keep carousing, much to the benefit of the owner's bottom line. It was a dive. It was a wonderful dive. Romantic and platonic relationships were forged on those barstools. Gripes about the silly kids and the stresses of responsibility made them more loveable when suds were swished with the laughter. Such an important place was the M-40 that several counselors made the trip to Decatur in October 2004 to celebrate Miner's fortieth birthday. There was no more perfect place than the M-40 for such an occasion.

Sometimes the staff would load up on liquor in town and bring it back to the public-access boat launch, located just past the camp property line, and drink there. One person made sure to play the radio in his or her car. Miner laid out the Magic Blanket and mixed Magic Cups of Jim Beam and Coke. Technically, the public access closed at dusk and this was illegal, and there were occasional raids by the Decatur fuzz. When this happened, many counselors scattered into the woods and made their way back to camp. Such was the case in 1998 when Doug took off in what became known as the "Run, Forrest, Run!" escape, forever earning the nickname "O.J." by those who were there.

Sisters Sophie and Rachel Terp were campers and counselors during the 1990s, and their family had a lake house twenty minutes up the road from camp in Paw Paw that became a popular spot. In 2000, a bar in Dowagiac called B.T.s replaced the Penny Lane as the place to go for dancing since no one was working the pole at Scooters.

> *"If you've never been the most important person in someone's life, you're about to be. Because what you say is going to mean more to them than what their parents say or their siblings say or their friends or anyone else, because you're their counselor."*
> *—Jeff Miner in his pre-camp training speech*

The time off and those evening hours were necessary. "There was a real division of old and new staff my last year of camp," Dan said. "I tried to get everyone to come together, but there was just this division, like 50/50 of old staff and new staff. Over the changeover weekend, we went to Windofest. Like 90 percent of the staff went to Windofest. And it was Windo's drunken mania that finally united all of us."

Although Windo wasn't a counselor in 1990, Dan asked him to host the annual changeover event. While the eight-week campers enjoyed a weekend trip away from camp at a water park and stayed in a hotel with the amenities

The staff taking advantage of some well-deserved R&R at Windofest '85. *Courtesy of Deb Bates.*

of cable TV and beds that didn't squeak, the counselors made their way to Mishawaka, Indiana, to Windo's house for a weekend of, well, anything. The exact goings-on are either top secret or blurred by the passing of time and consumption of booze.

Pairing up late at night, counselors from both sides of the road hunted the most secluded places to get close. Places like the teepee, the Riflery Range, the waterfront...any place that wasn't already occupied by another couple or would reduce the amount of mosquito bites on your butt.

As a nineteen-year-old first-time counselor, "Big" James Boulware didn't know what he was getting into. "The maintenance guy, Ken Olsen, made a point to say to me, 'It's cool to go out and drink. But when the kids are there, you best be able to do your job.'"

David Himmel trying to look the part. *Courtesy of Billy Hearth.*

And the counselors always did their jobs. Every director hired quality counselors, people who wanted to be there, and it showed. The counselors the kids lived with were the best. Of course, not every single staff member was an all-star. When Billy Hearth was the boys' program director in 1999, the staff was so bad that you could go to breakfast with someone and by lunch that person was fired. But the bums were very few and very far between.

Following my first summer at camp, I knew that I wanted to be a counselor. I wanted to be cool like that. I wanted to have friends like that. I wanted to go to that place called the M-40—whatever that was. I wanted the responsibility. I wanted to be to my campers what my counselors were to me; I wanted to be a hero. Because that's what counselors are.

Chapter 9

TURTLEMAN

Turtleman was a great way to scare the little kids. To me, it's like Santa Claus.
—Rory Zacher

Ask any person who went to any overnight summer camp anywhere, and they'll tell you that it was the best time of their life. They'll rattle off stories that are fun, funny and exciting. There's a bounty under that hot summer sun. But when the daylight goes and gives way to the darkness of wilderness, camp becomes a very different sort of place. It becomes scary. And any camp without a ghost story to complement those dark hours would be remiss.

In the late 1960s, Greenwoods Camp employed the meanest, most irresponsible and loathed counselor in its history. He was a beast of a man, made of pure muscle and mass. A trained killer compliments of the United States Army. A few years before, he had been dishonorably discharged because of several violent episodes. Apparently, he was too rough for even the military to handle.

He withheld campers' mail for sport or read affectionate letters between parents and kids out loud to the entire cabin just to embarrass. If there happened to be a homesick camper in the cabin, he teased the boy to tears. He stole his campers' comic books and anything he may have found interesting in a package from home. Sometimes he'd confiscate an entire package and destroy its contents right in front of the kid or walk to the Boys' Swim Dock and throw their personal belongings into the lake. He cursed at them. He yelled at them. He frightened them. He made camp a living hell.

The History of Lake of the Woods and Greenwoods Camps

One year, while a counselor in Comanche, a few of his campers were sent packages full of fireworks. It was nearing the Fourth of July, and packages of this sort were not uncommon. He immediately took the fireworks away from the campers and stashed them under his bed. That Fourth of July evening, after lights out, the counselor went down to the public access at the end of 47th1/2 Street and got drunk. He got absolutely wasted.

Just before curfew at 1:00 a.m., he stumbled into Comanche cabin with a freshly lit cigarette dangling from his mouth. He collapsed onto his bed and took a long drag of the cigarette, which left the end bright red and hot. He pinched the butt between his fingers and exhaled a plume of smoke as he pulled the cigarette away from his mouth before passing out.

Earlier that night, his campers had gone under his bed to sort through and reclaim their fireworks, but they scrambled back to their bunks when the OD came in for a bed check. They left the pyrotechnics in a jumbled heap barely tucked away. A few short minutes after passing out, the counselor's hand went limp, and the cigarette fell to the floor and rolled next to the explosives.

The cherry-red tip was still hot, and it torched a wick. A small box of smoke bombs ignited, which led the plastic and cardboard packaging to smolder and melt. Quickly, the rest of the contraband began to burn. Smoke filled the cabin. Several boys woke up confused but sure that something was wrong. Bottle rockets began to scream, and Roman candles shot bursts of fire into the rafters. Black Cats popped. Ground spinners, fountains, mines, snakes, strobes and wheels all began to burn and boom and bang and hiss.

Everyone in the cabin was now up, blinded by smoke and dazed by deafening concussions. The surrounding cabins' lights came on. But the despised Comanche counselor slept, too drunk to wake. And as fast as it began, his bed started to burn from underneath. The old, dry mattress was perfect kindling. His stiff blankets flamed with the speed of the bark from the paper birch tree. The wood paneling that his corner bed sat against began to scorch, and in a flash, the flames were devouring the counselor.

Just as his co-counselor came to his aid with the cabin's fire extinguisher, the man leaped up, a human pyre, and screamed. He shot through the cabin door and ran down the hill toward the lake as a large, red-hot blaze trailed him. He ran along the road to the girls' swim area. Several campers and counselors watched from shore, too amazed and terrified to take action as he threw himself into the lake and swam fast toward Turtle Bay just beyond the Ski Annex. His screams and flames did not immediately die when he entered the water, but eventually, the sight and sound of him was gone.

With the night quiet again, the counselors regained their senses and rushed into the water in an attempt to save what was left of their fellow counselor. But no one could find him. He was gone.

The following morning, Decatur authorities dispatched search parties. The entire bottom of Lake of the Woods was combed by divers, but the counselor's charred remains were never found. Additional search parties were sent through the surrounding woods of the campgrounds and into the migrant worker camps just down the road. Through cornfields and residential yards, bloodhounds and police looked for the counselor, but no one, nothing, could find him. Like smoke in the night, he had vanished.

The rest of the summer passed as any other before it. Activities resumed the next day, and repairs were made to Comanche cabin. If anything, following that horrific night, Greenwoods was a happier place because the counselor, that despicable man, was gone.

The following year's Carnival Day was the hottest day of the summer, and Sadie Hawkins encouraged love. For obvious reasons, fireworks were no longer allowed on campgrounds, but the day was still a blast. After the dance, both camps sat at the waterfront and watched Decatur's fireworks show. Everyone returned to the cabins, and taps was played. The camp fell gently to sleep.

Just before 1:00 a.m., as many of the staff returned from their night out, screams shattered the quiet night. Male counselors ran in the direction of the ruckus, all figuring that campers were making trouble. But when they threw open the doors of Comanche cabin, they found a horrific and otherworldly sight.

Beds and dressers were thrown about the cabin as if a rabid tornado had passed through. The twelve-year-old boys were all huddled in the far corner of the closet and screaming as if death was near. A dark, hulking beast towered over them. Several brave counselors lunged at the monster's back, but it shooed them off with its swinging elbows, sending them against either side of the cabin, shattering the windows from the force. The monster grabbed a boy by his head, the way one would palm a basketball, and burst through the other counselors standing at the door like they were Japanese paper walls.

The boy pleaded for help through throat-tearing screams as the monster ran toward the lake. The counselors chased it. A few caught up to it and grabbed on to an arm, a leg or its back. But they, too, were quickly shrugged off. The monster ran into the lake and submerged fast with the boy in tow. For a moment, it was silent. But more counselors came, and more than a dozen dove into the lake to keep chase. There was a struggle. More screaming and yelling, and again it went quiet.

The counselors lost the monster and the boy. They asked one another in astonishment, "Where did it go?" "Where are they?" "Are you okay?" Suddenly, the captured boy shot through the water's surface as if propelled by a rocket from below. His entire body spun above the counselors before splashing down.

He was safe and not seriously injured, but he was rattled and quite worse for the wear. He spent three days and nights in the Infirmary, along with the two counselors who were thrown in the cabin. Again the Decatur authorities searched for this alleged monster but came up with nothing.

The counselors who wrestled with the monster that night testified to its enormous size and incredible strength. They said it reeked of sulfur, and its skin was black and felt reptilian or burned. It was soaking wet and seemed to be waterlogged the way the skin would squish like wringing out a wet sponge. No counselor got a clear look at its face, but the Comanche boys who had to stare into it while it chose its victim from the closet said that it had wide, black eyes and no nose or lips. It looked like a vicious turtle. Because of these features, the monster was aptly named Turtleman.

It is said that Turtleman is the undead abomination of the counselor who was consumed by the flames of fireworks in Comanche cabin. It's believed that he lives in Turtle Bay, a popular destination for canoeing classes because of its shallow waters and many sunbathing turtles. Lake of the Woods is a mud-bottom lake, and this is nowhere more evident than in Turtle Bay, where canoers can stick their paddles into the bottom and have them sink down as far as they can reach. There are very few spots of solid ground in Turtle Bay. The interesting part about it is the stink of sulfur in the air. It becomes more potent when paddling disturbs the mud. And each Fourth of July, Turtleman returns to Comanche cabin to devour the flesh of a camper in hopes of replacing his own human skin.

I was nearly a victim of Turtleman. It was 1991, my second year at camp, and I was in Comanche cabin. It was the Fourth of July dance, and I was grooving away on the stage when the backstage door burst open and I was snatched from behind and pulled down to the lake.

I don't remember screaming, but I remember how large the hand felt as it squeezed my skull while carrying me. I remember the stench of rotten eggs, an odor commonly associated with sulfur. I remember how grainy and tough, but wet, his skin felt when my hand brushed against his leg. I remember thinking, "This is it. This is Turtleman and he's going to kill me."

He dragged me into the water near Timber Trails and began swimming across the lake toward Turtle Bay before letting me go. I assume the counselors who chased us down scared him off. I was quickly pulled on shore before passing out from fear. I woke up in the Infirmary, with my younger brother, Eric, kneeling at my bedside, crying his eyes out, wailing to God not to let me die.

Two days later, I was asked to say a few words during lunchtime announcements just to let everyone know I was fine.

That story is true…except that my kidnapping was a setup. The entire stunt was the brainchild of the assistant director, Dawn. It was predetermined that I would be dancing on the stage at that precise moment. My cue, we decided, would be when the deejay played "Poison" by Bell Biv DeVoe, a hugely popular song that would certainly crowd the dance floor with witnesses. At the second verse, a Mohawk named David Ladowitz, dressed in a full body wetsuit and black makeup and lathered in sand, dirt and seaweed, would throw open the backstage door, pick me up and run with me down to the lake, where I would float near the shore at Timber Trails while he swam off to the other side of the waterfront to change out of costume and return to the rest of the camp.

The counselors all knew about it, so there was no real alarm. It was a perfectly choreographed gag that seemed to have enough people tricked into thinking that Turtleman had risen again. It was harmless and pretty funny. In fact, it took everything I had to not crack up when Eric was bawling at my bedside.

But there's no way a trick like that could ever be pulled today. We've become too sensitive. In fact, ghost stories are outlawed at camp now, the same as fireworks and peanut butter, because no child should be frightened or intimidated by the imagination of something scary lurking in the night.

However, the story must be told. It must be repeated in hushed tones under blankets with flashlights or among creaky trees, their shadows dancing like wild demons with the flames of the campfire. Ghost stories are a part of the camp experience. It is a camper's nature to host irrational fears and test one another's bravery against the unknown, the absurd and the Turtleman.

Chapter 10
COLOR DAYS

Color Days are for fun. Color Days are for you to test your skills. Color Days will help you find out what kind of person you are.
—Greenwoods Camp Color Days motto, 1980–81

There is no time at camp more revered, more wrought with excitement and anxiety, than the final three days of the summer. And there's no time at camp that affects more people in a deeper, personal way. Those days are known as Color Days.

The camps are split into two teams. Each team gets a counselor as an advisor and two senior campers to serve as the coveted captains. The remaining campers are divvied up evenly by athletic prowess, activity skills and personality. For the next three days, the two teams compete in events ranging from team competitions like flag football to individual events like the lake swim.

Points are earned by winning the obvious competitions, as well as lineup and individual inspection at flag and before meals, cabin cleanup, the team flag for the girls and the plaque for the boys. Even packing to go home earns points. The team song and cheer, as well as the capture the flag game on the second night, are ways the entire team can work together. The big point earner—and the crux of Color Days—is teamwork. There are also the guideposts of Color Days known as the Seven Virtues. They are friendship, determination, sportsmanship, tolerance, enthusiasm, patience and unity.

The days' competitions culminate with the Obstacle Relay. Every single camper must participate in this regardless of skill level, which is why there

The Blue Team captains and advisor watch as the rope catches fire. *Courtesy of Lindsay Saewitz.*

are events like pie eating and solving a math problem. The relay is complete and Color Days is over when one of the teams builds a fire and burns a piece of twine strung between two wooden posts about two feet off the ground. Building the fire and burning the rope first is the equivalent of knocking a grand slam out of the park with two outs and a full count in the final inning to win the World Series.

It is a simple enough premise, but it stirs up emotions and competitive drive that would make the gladiators of ancient Rome drop their swords, sit back with the lions and say, "Now this is entertainment. This is competition. This is passion. These children bleed their team colors."

The girls' teams have always been blue and white, representing the camp's colors. Greenwoods teams were at first orange and brown. In 1964, though, Dan Langell changed them to red and black. Because really, when you look at orange and brown together, they resemble fecal matter more than anything.

Because boys are usually more prone to developing a blood thirst during competition, the intense red and black colors may have initiated the evolution into a more warlike Color Days. The 1970 Greenwoods Camp Color Days packet has written inside, "Color Days should help you find out: What kind of teammate you are. What kind of sportsman you are. What kind of friend you are. What kind of person you are. You will find out the most by trying the hardest." By 1983, the following dialogue from Shakespeare's *Julius Caesar* was written on the cover of the Color Days packet: "There is a tide in the affairs of men, which taken at flood, leads on to fortune; omitted, all the voyage of their life is bound in the shallows and the miseries. On such a full sea we are now afloat, and we must take the current when it serves, or lose our ventures." In any English literature class, this can be understood as "it's best to take advantage of your enemies when they are down and you have the advantage, or else you could lose everything."

The Color Days event was designed as an opportunity to put to use that which had been learned during the summer—from making your bed to paddling a canoe, from clearing a table to building a controlled fire and burning a rope…all put to the tune of friendly, natural, human competition.

The Color Days Opening Ceremony for the boys is dramatic, both in practice and in emotion. The lead up to the ceremony has always been the same. About an hour after lights out, counselors wake their cabins, and the boys are instructed to remain completely quiet and to line up in flag formation. From there, staff with torches made of kerosene-soaked toilet paper rolls inside coffee cans, nailed to three-foot-long two-by-four boards, escort the boys along a luminary-lined path toward the bonfire.

When it was held at the Boys' Campfire, it began several ways: a skilled archer shooting a flaming arrow into the wood to ignite the fire or a zip line wire from the tree carrying a flaming roll of toilet paper into the kerosene-soaked woodpile. Additional ceremonial flair included loudspeakers set up across the lake on the Point that announced the advisors, captains and teams, as well as a floating object in the lake made of chicken wire and kerosene-sodden sanitary napkins spelling out "Color Days" in flames.

When the property around the lake became popularized in the 1980s, fires in the water and loudspeakers were not feasible; as a result, the ceremony was moved to the golf range, where a massive fire can be built. The ceremony remains here today. The heat is impressive. From the size and amount of wood used, one might wonder what part of camp has been deforested.

Select counselors and the program director serve as the Color Days Committee and meet the camp at the fire wearing their committee T-shirts. Two smaller fires on separate sides of the bonfire burn for each team, with four flags, two for each team, in cement-filled coffee cans. Beside them are bamboo frames painted the color of the corresponding team that hold enough torn red and black cloth for each team member to tie at least one ribbon around one of his wrists. Once all the cabins are lined up, the program director says a few words about sportsmanship, teamwork and the other Seven Virtues. Two other committee members begin reading the teams. Red advisor. Black advisor. Red captain. Black captain. Red captain. Black captain…and then the rest of the teams are read off by age-appropriate divisions like Seniors, Upper Intermediates, Lower Intermediates and Juniors.

When the teams are assembled, the program director releases them back to their cabins as teams, marching single file and not uttering a sound until after breakfast the following morning. Only advisors and captains are permitted to speak, as well as stay out until midnight at the Mess Hall strategizing the coming days. Although the captains have three days of fight ahead of them, it's hard not to bask in glory sitting in the Mess Hall late at night with staff members socializing with one another all around you. You feel like something bigger, and as a Color Days captain, you are.

The cut-and-dry earnestness of the Greenwoods Color Days Opening Ceremony has made way for a more flamboyant display. The last few years have witnessed intense performances by the committee members wherein they act out a short play with costumes and props. In 2011, I visited camp and attended the first opening ceremony I'd seen in eleven years. I scribbled down the following as it occurred:

> *The walk along the illuminated path was the same as it had been for decades. Little brown paper bags filled with sand and a small tea candle line the path from the cabin area to the back end of the golf range. The boys are quiet, but not as quiet as I remember being. A 50-foot wooden stack dwarfed the teepee. Then, the banging of tin drums. What was this noise? Was it the Grove camp? Townies? From the darkness, a scream. Some sort of warrior emerged. A counselor dressed like a gladiator. Horses are also in costume. Camp is Rome's Colosseum.*

The evolution was inevitable. It was 2006, and Rob Burns was a first-year counselor by way of England. He was good. He was in the youngest cabin, and the kids liked him. The staff liked him, too. At the end of the summer, boys' program director Mike Billingsley had to leave a few days early. He stayed to open Color Days and then headed out with the rest of the committee at the wheel. Though still green, the Big House appointed

Rob interim program director. "I was given [the files], and I still didn't know exactly what was going on," Rob said. And that's because Greenwoods traditions can be difficult to wrap your head around if you haven't been through them at least once. Although he had served on the Olympic Days Committee the previous session, Color Days was a different beast entirely.

"We were a team of program directors really," Rob said about the Color Days Committee members. "As a committee, we made decisions, and we all worked together to come up with new approaches and ideas." Rob and the rest of the committee did think it odd that the winner of Color Days was so plainly announced. The program director ceremoniously balled up the total scores, tossed them into the fire and then named the winning team. "I wanted us to come up with a dramatic way to announce the winner after this dramatic event," said Rob. "I thought it'd be great for the kids to tell their parents, 'They did this cool…thing!' But the next day, a kid asked me why. 'Why would you change this?'"

Now the boys' full-time program director ever since, Rob and his staff spend an incredible amount of time coming up with new ways to close Color Days as well as Olympic Days, like having two jugs on standby at the rope burning. One is filled with kerosene and the other with juice. The jugs are poured simultaneously over the teams' rope fires. The winner's fire flames up and the loser's turns to smoke. But it's getting harder to come up with new ideas. By 2009, a less pyrotechnic committee placed medals around the winning captains' necks. And Rob received an e-mail from a camper saying that he didn't like it. "When you set the bar, you can't go back. It becomes the new expectation," Rob said. For kids, tradition comes quickly. And it's always a risk to change it.

No matter how theatrical the opening ceremony may have been, whether it was a flaming raft, a beastly bonfire or a one-act play with counselors dressed as ninjas breaking Styrofoam boards (as it was in 2009), one thing was certain: the moment the teams were called out, the camp became militant.

"There was no rebellion, no pushback," said Dan, the Black Team captain in 1986 with Mark Podl. "Everybody would fall in line for the captains. There was nothing better than walking into the Iroquois or Sioux cabins and getting such respect and seeing the way they trusted that you would lead them to a victory."

At Lake of the Woods, the girls are woken up and line up silently outside their cabins before walking in a single-file line along the illuminated path to the hill of the Archery Range, where they sit and face the lake. There is no burning fire to greet them. The only light is from the torches that a counselor from each cabin holds as they stand at the water facing the girls. The program director calls out for the White and Blue spirits, who are Color Days Committee members waiting on the hill. The spirits make their way to the bottom of the hill, where a kind of staged reading ensues. "I am the spirit of the White. I represent the clouds of a summer's day, white caps on the water." Then, "I am the spirit of the Blue. I represent the sky, running waters and the happiness of the bluebird."

The program director then lights the reasonably sized bonfire. Each cabin's counselors step forward to symbolically add their flames to the fire. The Seven Virtues are represented and explained by a decades-old traditional script, while the program director, or sometimes Dayna, lights alternating blue and white candles in a seven-stick candelabra. The girls then take a vow of silence until flag raising the next morning after breakfast and cabin cleanup.

Select committee members then walk behind the line of counselors and place whistles on lanyards over the heads of the two advisors. From there it's up to the top of the hill, where the Bryn Mawrs sit, many stifling sniffles and tears and anticipation. Whistles are placed over the heads of the two Blue and two White captains. The cries become audible, and the captains take their places with their advisors and begin reading off their team members' names. Then it's a quiet walk back to the cabin to try and sleep while the captains and advisors head to the Mess Hall to celebrate the honor and start planning.

There is an undying loyalty campers have to their team and color. Once you are chosen for the Red, Black, White or Blue Team, you will stay on that team with hopes of becoming that team's captain your senior year. Your siblings, cousins, nephews, nieces, children, grandchildren and so on will more than likely wear your color. This can exacerbate the competitive nature of Color Days. So when Laura Hollander Gill, a Blue Team captain in 1966, picked up her daughter, Holly Gill Jacobs, at the end of the summer nearly thirty years later and learned that she was on the White Team, Laura was appalled. Holly went on to become a White Team captain, much to her mother's conflicted pride for sure.

If there is a team change, it's for a good reason, and it usually only happens in order for a senior camper to be a captain. Such was the case with Bob in 1990. There were four senior Mohawks: Bob, Mike Camodeca and twin brothers Adam and Derek Shaf. Bob and the Shafs were traditionally Blacks, and it was unspeakable to even consider pitting brother against brother.

"That whole summer, I looked forward to being a Color Days captain— frankly my whole camp career, like most long-term campers," Bob said. "I was always on Black, so I assumed that is where I would be. Near the end of the summer, a counselor, I don't remember who, came up to me and asked, 'Would you prefer to stay on Black or switch to Red and be a captain?' I didn't even hesitate. Right away I said, 'Switch to Red.' In the camp world, nothing was more important to me than being a Color Days captain." It was a good move; he and Camodeca took Red to a victory.

Switches like that are rare. Even less common is a thirteen-year-old being a captain. But in 1963, when Linda was in Pembroke, she was picked to lead the White Team. "It was very surprising," she said. "And next year, when I should have been captain, I wasn't. But it was good because I could help the other captains with what I had learned the year before."

Loyal to her White Team as its leader, Linda never thought twice about what color team she was on. From the Greenberg era and well into Seegerville, team colors and team members at Lake of the Woods were interchangeable from summer to summer. There was the opening ceremony at night, during which the advisors and captains were chosen, but not for one specific color or team. The next morning, the captains convened in the rec lodge for a coin toss. The captain who won the toss chose between picking a team color or an envelope containing the team rosters. So the teams were already chosen without a color in mind. In 1964, Laura won the coin toss and chose the Blue Team because she happened to have been on Blue before.

By the late 1980s and early '90s, the girl captains spent the hours after the ceremony walking through the cabins with their team rosters tying white or blue cloth around the foot of the beds so when the camper woke up, she discovered what team she was on. Also by this time, the once-a-certain-color-always-a-certain-color tradition was in place.

Team allegiances exist across the road as well. Somewhere along the timeline, White and Red, as well as Blue and Black, became brother and sister teams. Occasionally this worked out to be a literal relationship, as in the case of Michelle Simms (Blue) and her younger brother Jacob (Black). But then there was the case of the Shaf family. Remember that brothers Adam and Derek were loyal Black Team members and co-captains in 1990. Well, they were just two-fourths of quadruplets, with their sisters Tiffany and Vanessa across the road. The girls were longtime White Team members and also co-captains in 1990. True to a color or not, there are no official, camp-sanctioned brother/sister teams.

"There are two things you aspire to be: Arrowhead and Color Days captain," said Dan. There is no greater pressure that comes before being named a captain and no higher honor felt when you are. For Alice, being a Color Days captain was a turning point for her. She was not competitive or athletic. Sure she could write poems, but for what? She was chosen as the White Team captain and led her team to a win. "Being a captain made me feel like I had something to give," she said.

"I thought that was such a fabulous compliment to me," Linda said about being a captain. "I felt recognized for leadership abilities, and not everyone got that, so it was special."

In the 1960s and '70s, the boys were told ahead of the opening ceremony that they would be captains. That took the pressure off but not the honor. It was the ultimate carrot on a stick. By nature, Tod pushed boundaries and flirted with trouble. He snuck out, he was a womanizer and he challenged authority. But by his senior Mohawk year, it was clear that he was a true leader. He was also better at not getting caught. Either way, he proved himself enough to earn captain. And his Red Team won.

Captains are chosen by their peers on both sides of the road. A week before Color Days, the senior campers cast a ballot vote. Counselors lend their opinions, and the Color Days Committee does as well, but captains are chosen, without question, in a populist vote. Placing the whistles over the girls' heads is a longstanding tradition at Lake of the Woods. The boys' Color Days Committee always called the names out. In 2011, however, they adopted a version of what the girls do, but instead of just walking behind the boys and placing the whistle around the neck of the chosen boy, a committee member paced behind them, exciting nerves and teasing anxiety before bestowing the honor.

During Color Days, counselors enjoy a lax couple of days overseeing and refereeing events. The Color Days Committees are like project heads and spend the remaining time playing pranks on one another—harmless pranks like the boys putting the goat in the girls' program director's cabin. The campers are the hard workers throughout Color Days. And this is no truer than for the captains.

With as much of their team's colors covering their bodies as possible, a clipboard in hand and a whistle in mouth, the captains' work is never

ORANGE AND BROWN   MEDLEY RELAY   1955 Season

RULES

1. You cannot use a person more than twice.

2. A runner is permitted to run the baton from one place to another. A person may act as a runner only once throughout the relay.

3. Acting as a runner does not count as using a man once.

4. The Baton must be presented to staff member in charge of event before event starts.

5. Each team hand in to Dave Farber a list of the boys in each event and no change may be made on this list after relay starts.

THE MEDLEY RELAY

1. The start of the race in a Shuttle Relay. Each man to run 30 yds. The relay to be held in center of Athletic Field.

2. The baton then goes to the Flag Pole Area where two boys will volley a ping pong ball across pingpong table back and forth to a count of 20.

3. The baton then goes to waterfront where two canoeists will hand paddle a canoe around a designated course set up by waterfront staff.

4. The baton is then taken up to Junior Softball Diamond where a boy runs around the bases two times.

5. A division of teams is now made at this point in race:
ORANGE BATON will be taken to riflery range where one man must score 30 points or better in 5 shots on a single bull target. The shooter must be in the group classified as 2nd best in riflery.

BROWN BATON will be taken to archery range where he must score____ points. All arrows must be returned by the archer to the staff member before the baton is sent on its way.

6. Carry baton to Girl's Pier where two boys are waiting to paddle a canoe to Boys Pier.

7. Hand baton to boy on Boy's diving board who hands it to staff member and then he dives off board and swims free style around the raft once then hands baton to

8. Boy on raft who hands baton to staff member on raft and then swims to shore, he tags boy on shore

9. Who jumps in boat and rows to raft to get baton and then rows back and hands baton to

10. Boy waiting on shore who runs baton to boys Campfire sight where 2 boys will be a fire, take the cans of water which will be supplied them, place soap in water, and remain until water boils over the can. No reflective materials may be used.

Page one of the 1955 Color Days Medley Relay Rules. This was the final Color Days relay to occur during the Greenberg era. The boys' colors were still orange and brown. *Courtesy of Lake of the Woods and Greenwoods Camps.*

done. They are the last ones to sleep at night and the first ones up in the morning. They play the hardest and cheer the loudest, and at the end of the three days, they are left hoarse, battered, exhausted and not regretting a single minute of it.

"We did the Obstacle Relay and wiped them out," Dan remembered.

> *But we couldn't get the fire to light. Red got their fire lit first and burned the rope, and in my entire time at camp, I'd never seen anyone lose the [obstacle] course and win.*
>
> *I remember sitting at that large tree just behind the Sail Dock shed. If I'd been alone, I would have been in tears. Lough came up to me and sat down and told me not to worry about it. He said something that made me think I might have this one…when they announced Black won, I was sitting by the tree.*
>
> *Someone told me, I think they were on the Color Days Committee, someone told me later, that we had it in the bag a day before. We swept song and cheer. Our song was to "Shout."*

One of Rory's greatest memories was his first year as captain of the Red Team with Linda's son, Jonathan. "We won. I didn't think we were going to because we lost the Obstacle Relay. We just didn't burn the rope in time, and Black was going crazy. When they announced the winner as the Red Team, I think I jumped higher than I ever have."

"The experience is so impossible to get anyone else to relate to—and that's winning Color Days as a captain," Dan said.

At the end of the Obstacle Relay, everyone cries, even the winners—even the boys. You are happy and relieved and tired, and sometimes you hurt for the other team, which has to watch you celebrate. Even after a winner is announced and the rope fires are put out, the captains are revered by campers and counselors alike. They have the opportunity to say a few words and accept awards from the camp director.

I was awarded the MVP, something I never saw before or since. The program director that year, Troy, handed me the red baton used in capture the flag and during the Obstacle Relay. The next day, I took the quartered broom handle that made the baton to the maintenance shed and sawed it in half. I kept one half, and I gave the other to my co-captain, Andrew Silverman. Our team lost, but man did we try. And if I could have, I would have cut that baton into enough pieces for every Red Team member. I don't remember, but I feel I said something to that end in my speech.

The efforts of a Color Days captain affect more than the individual. The song competition in 1965 changed the entire "Greenwoods Camp Song." Before 1966, the song was called "On Camp Greenwoods" and was set to the tune of the University of Wisconsin–Madison's "On Wisconsin." However, one of the competitions during Color Days was to not just sing the camp song but also to write one and perform it. So, in 1965, Shelly wrote a song for the Black Team to the Northwestern University fight song. It was a hit. But it wasn't until the next summer when "On Camp Greenwoods" was replaced.

"I wrote the song over the winter because I was sure I was going to be the Black Team captain," Shelly said. "I wrote the lyrics to the Notre Dame fight song—a [predominantly] Jewish camp singing the tune of Notre Dame? It was kind of funny. But I also thought that when it comes to competition, the more shtick you can put in, the better. And the Notre Dame song had two verses. The first was sung, and the second was done in a whisper. Everyone loved it, and Dan Langell had us teach it to the camp. We just copied the shtick. And it all came out of trying to win Color Days."

Big James was the advisor for the Red Team in 1998 and had just suffered a loss when he said in his speech, "No matter how hard things get, remember how hard you tried."

Those are words to live by. During Color Days, we are forced to reach down and find the best of what we are made of. If you worked hard during Color Days, you delivered something deep and true. Maybe more than you ever will. And that's something to remember in those later years.

Out of all of the traditions that have come, gone and stayed over the last nearly eight decades, Color Days is the one that remains closest to its original form. It has swayed, moved, adjusted and adapted, but it remains the three days when a kid becomes the person he or she is destined to be.

Chapter II

A CAMPER IN THE BIG HOUSE

Change alone is eternal, perpetual, immortal.
—*Arthur Schopenhauer*

Dayna loved her day camp. But by 1979, a lot of girls from Chicago's North Shore were attending Lake of the Woods Camp, and she figured, why not? Laurie came to her house with his carousel slide projector and gave his spiel—she was sold. On the bus up to camp, she and her friend, whom she looked an awful lot like, decided that they would dress as twins every day for the next four weeks.

The next summer, it was the same thing. Day camp for the first half and then overnight camp. As she got older, cheerleading camp replaced day camp, and when she was fourteen, she ran her own day camp out of her backyard for the kids on her block during the first four weeks of summer. It was all camp all the time. She did have to skip her senior Bryn Mawr year at Lake of the Woods because of cheerleading, but she was back in Decatur and back in the saddle in 1985.

Because Dayna took to riding so quickly her first year of camp, by the time she was a junior counselor she was a seasoned pro and ideal for teaching it. She alternated between the stables and Ski Dock that year, but as a full-blown counselor, she was a riding instructor. "I never should have told them I rode," she said laughing. "Because once they find out you're good at riding, you're stuck there. It's much harder to find good riding instructors than good skiing instructors."

The History of Lake of the Woods and Greenwoods Camps

By 1991, Dayna was twenty-two and had been at Lake of the Woods for twelve summers. In college, her dream career was to either be a rock-and-roll singer or a camp owner and director. "I always said that the chance that someone is cut out to be a camp director is pretty slim. But when I became program director and assistant director and realized you could work year round…once I did that, I knew. I knew that's what I wanted to do."

Still, when she left Marc after the 1994 summer, she was at peace with her decision. She married the charming Terry Hardin, and they moved to Scottsdale, Arizona, where he worked in radio sales while Dayna finished her master's degree in education. She never wanted to teach, but she liked the psychology of it, which is not surprising having spent most of her life at camp.

At the pool of the apartment complex where the Hardins were renting while house-hunting, Dayna met the CFO of a small tech company that had just been bought by Viacom. The company was developing a new technology for the classroom. "I was blown away," she said. "They were beaming live TV into classrooms across the globe. Think about all the public schools that didn't have any resources, and suddenly the kids were interacting with a real historian and talking to Ted Danson about *Gulliver's Travels* because he just finished shooting the movie."

A week later she interviewed for a position not knowing what it was or what she'd be doing. When they offered it to her, she accepted it immediately. "I went there, did a few projects, and the next thing I knew, I was in charge of all the content for all the channels." She was asked to build more, and it was exciting for her; she was twenty-six years old and a vice-president of an innovative, educational tech company.

"I was so young. And I just kept thinking, 'It was camp that taught me those leadership skills, it was camp that taught me how to work with people and talk with people.' Everything was transferrable."

So this was her life. Not even thirty, a VP living in Scottsdale with a husband and a life of possibilities as expansive as the Valley of the Sun. Then the phone rang.

"I want to sell," the voice said.

Dayna always told Marc to call her if he ever wanted to unload the camp. He had approached the topic four years before, but she turned it down because she felt she was too young. So he called her again. The Hardins talked it over. Terry was onboard, and suddenly what was past was prologue. Dayna was going to trade her high-profile gig for the dream of camp directing. She was about to become a different kind of rock star.

The Big House, circa 2000. *Courtesy of Lake of the Woods and Greenwoods Camps.*

The new Big House, 2011. *Photo by David Himmel.*

Getting money to pay for the camp wasn't easy. Banks don't like giving loans for summer camps because they're high-risk investments. Not high-risk in a dangerous sort of way, but rather there's loads of overhead. And if enrollment drops, tuition drops. And if tuition drops, income to pay the bank loan drops, too. Dayna, Terry and Marc worked out a deal in which Marc acted as the bank. They closed the sale on October 10, 1997. Marc handed her one application. There was one kid enrolled.

The changing of the guard was announced to cheers at the 1997 reunion a month later. Many of the families knew Dayna from her previous summers, and there was certainty that she was the best person for the job. She was a little apprehensive, however, about how she was going to run a boys' camp and how she would even recruit boys to the camp. The girl knew her Lake of the Woods, but Greenwoods was a familiar stranger. "But it ended up being a great thing because every boys' camp needs a camp mom," she said.

Things changed quickly when Dayna moved into the Big House. Marc may have started the modernization of the camp's business model by introducing the Internet to daily practices, but Dayna dropped it into the next gear. The camp needed kids and fast. She immediately exercised her charm and business acumen, and though there was just one kid on the roster in October, the first Hardin summer saw about 375 kids go through.

"The thing about Lake of the Woods and Greenwoods is that your reputation precedes you," Dayna said. "Even if enrollment wasn't good at the time, it was huge in the 1950s, '60s and '70s. It was *the* camp to go to. All of that contributes to it being built back up."

Just like Laurie started making over the camp in 1956, Dayna did the same in 1998. The property needed a lot of work. One thing that can be said for every owner is that each one added on, made improvements and adapted to the changing times. But buildings that go unused nine months out of the year have a way of taking a beating. "They were never kept up," Dayna said. "We'd clean them before we closed, but we'd open and they'd be filthy. Marc had one caretaker and not a good one—Marc knows that. He used to be a principal at the school, so it was like a part-time job. Then he hired Mike Conover in 1996, and Mike was a great addition."

There was a long list to work from, but if she changed everything at once, she'd have a revolt on her hands; tradition can be tangible. Besides, she didn't have the cash flow needed to overhaul everything. So she thought about the kids. "What would the kids and parents notice? Because unfortunately, a lot of what you spend money on doesn't get seen, like septic or new ovens in the kitchen. So I started with remodeling the cabins."

As assistant director, she oversaw the beginning of this project when pine wood paneling was added to the Greenwoods cabins. In '98, she finished the job. She replaced every toilet in camp. She looked at the little things, too, like painting and replacing picnic benches. She bought new ski boats and replaced sailboats that had been taking on water since the '70s. It's not that the place was a dump or that the equipment wasn't useable or unsafe; no, not at all. It's that camp needed a spit shine.

From the opening day, it was clear that a new sheriff was in town. Dayna staffed that summer with a lot of familiar faces from her years as a counselor. Many of the kids she taught to ride were old enough to drive ski boats, like Stacey Borden, David Ladowitz and Rory Zacher, or teach sports and be the Mohawk counselor, like Doug Bates. That first summer, it seemed, she surrounded herself with allies, friends who knew the camp she knew and would help her usher in the new era with ease.

The help was nice. Not only did Dayna have a new camp with new projects filling every inch of hers and Conover's to-do list, she had a new family, too. Dayna and Terry's son, Dylan, came along in December 1998. Now think about that for a moment. It's your first summer running your new camp, and you're six months pregnant…impressive. Dylan's addition gave good reason for Dayna to build her house in the woods. But clearing out a fair chunk of the woods next to the Girls' Campfire Circle in 1999 caused a stir among returning staff and campers. There were hushed accusations that she was turning camp into a country club. Miner said it best when he said, "If *you* owned gorgeous lakefront property, wouldn't *you* want to build a house on it?" The Big House was home to many babies over the years. But by the dawn of the new millennium, its slanting walls and sloped floors were no longer ideal for an infant. Plus, Miner had a point. And her family continued to grow when son Tyler came around four years later.

It wasn't the only grief thrown around about the aesthetic changes she was making in her early years. When the totem pole was erected at the waterfront in 2000, some were up in arms over it. "Why would she put a totem pole up? Camp never had a totem pole," some protested. But of course, camp *did* have a totem pole during Seegerville. She wasn't so much making a change as she was restoring tradition.

The changes Dayna made may have left the stubborn annoyed, but she was doing great things for the camp name, the business and, above all, the kids. New equipment continued to show up. Every summer was like Christmas morning, but for mostly Jewish kids. The Climbing Wall and Ropes Course were built. A budding national radio program did an entire show about summer camp and featured Lake of the Woods and Greenwoods. *This American Life*'s "Notes on Camp" has ranked as one of the top favorite shows since it was first broadcast in 1998. It receives regular airplay several times a year. Kids come to the camp knowing little more than what Ira Glass and Julie Snyder reported on the program. Dayna was right; the camp's reputation was preceding itself.

The demand for a bigger camp came first. With updated marketing material and a nationally syndicated radio show out there, kids were coming in droves. The girls had ten cabins in 1998, and today there are thirteen. The boys had nine cabins then. One of those was the small Cheyenne cabin. In 2000, the storage/program director's cabin was torn down, and Kiowa was built. Cheyenne has since been the permanent cabin for the program director, or directors as the case may be. Two more cabins were built, one of which even had an addition put on, now called the annex. There are eleven cabins on the boys' side, and the two newest ones have their own showers.

Greenwoods Camp cabin area in 2011. *Photo by David Himmel.*

As the number of campers increased, the old buildings just weren't big enough. The original Louis Lodge was torn down, and the larger Bob's Lodge, named after Dayna's father, was built in 2003. The boys were treated to a larger shower house, with its own counselor section. This shower house has individual stalls with full-coverage curtains and faucets, a major upgrade from the old house that had no temperature control or strings or chains to pull down and hook to the wall through an eyelet screw. Having washable pressure and palpable heat was a crapshoot in prior years. However, there's no denying the charm and campiness of that old mold factory.

Size and aesthetics were the minutiae. Cultural changes were the real matters. Life was simpler without the Internet. The new age made marketing and hiring easier, but it caused a crack in the dome that kept camp away from the outside world. Before, kids were lucky if they saw a newspaper—not that they wanted to. But operating a camp in a post-9/11 world of heightened anxiety and the societal dependence on social networking sites and immediate communication tools like texting and cellphone calls, the expectations from the parents are much greater. They want to see their kids, hear how camp is going and be updated on

The original Girls' Rec Lodge. *Courtesy of Lake of the Woods and Greenwoods Camps.*

Bob's Lodge. See the Canteen on the left side of the building. *Photo by David Himmel.*

happenings constantly. These variables made for a new kind of family—one navigated by the helicopter parent.

"When we went to camp, parents didn't call; they just didn't call," Dayna said. "You got a bad letter? So what, you got a bad letter. We have had to hire many additional people just to work with our parents. That, combined with our social media efforts and parents expecting e-mails in the middle of the night…It's just more complicated." But this isn't a complaint. And it's handled quite well. If nothing else, expanding parental demands have led to a job boom at camp. And in a down economy, that's a good thing.

Campers used to risk everything to sneak over to Timber Trails and call home on the park's pay phone. Dunes trips required a counselor to be on phone duty to keep kids from calling home. Now the concern is not the kids going *out* to make phone calls but rather smuggling cellphones *in*. It's not that camp directors want to prevent communication; it's that if a child has constant contact with mom and dad, camp kind of doesn't work. Today, the challenge is showing the kids that independence is possible when, in decades past, independence helped the kids unpack. It was just there, waiting for them. Because of helicopter parenting, kids come to camp with fewer coping skills. While it's always been a place to build or improve those skills, there's more starting from scratch than before. So really, camp is needed now more than ever.

Here's the thing. Helicopter parents mean well and only have the best intentions. But they are so quick to save their kids while at home that any trouble in the cabin has to be dealt with swiftly by the Big House. When I was a camper, we used to truck our cabin mates. This was when several boys snuck up on a sleeping kid at night with two flashlights as headlights and pillows as the truck. They'd all yell, "Truck!" as loud as they could, which woke the sleeper up to see two headlights followed by a swift beating with the pillows. It was all in good fun, but there's no way that would be tolerated today. Neither would a garbage truck or a boat. These are the same as a basic truck but also involved trash or water being dumped on the sleeping kid.

Still, boys tease and fight, girls roll their eyes and exclude. But each camper signs a bully contract at the beginning of camp, and it outlines the consequences of cruel behavior. Punishments aren't the same anymore either. No boy will be told to hug a tree, lay spread-eagle facedown on the ground with his arms and legs out or sit in his skivvies under the program cabin light to be devoured by mosquitoes. Punishment for Tod in his day was guarding the flagpole at night—standing in the dark, holding two brooms at arms' length, not moving, like a British Royal Guard but in underpants. My Chippewa counselor, Greg Perkins, threw me in the lake on the very last day of camp because I accidentally woke him up before the announcement came on. Again, there's no way that could happen today. This is how society adapts. It's also how campers stay dry.

Being a camper may be different this generation than before, but so is being a counselor. "We didn't bring cellphones or communicate on Facebook," DC said. "And when you ask twenty-year-old counselors to give up that connectivity, that's asking a lot." Counselor curfews are earlier. Nights in don't mean spending time out of the cabin hanging out in the Mess Hall instead of heading to the M-40; they mean the counselors stay in the cabin all night with their kids. Of course, having counselors on a tighter schedule makes it harder to sneak out. But kids aren't doing that anyway. "We had to get strict with that," Dayna said. "It's not like they're just holding hands anymore."

The way kids respond to the opposite sex is different. "We used to do Circle in the dark," said DC. "Now it's in the Pavilion with the lights on." Even the dynamics of the Bryn Mawr/Mohawk Trip have changed. "We needed the whole afternoon to get ready. Mike Conover knew he'd have to reset the power because we were going to blow fuses with all of our hair dryers and curling irons."

The Miller Pavilion is used for the Drama Show, Staff Show, Bryn Mawr Show and others. It hosts Circle as well as dances. In 2008, it held the reception for the wedding of two counselors who had met and married at camp, Christine O'Connell and Ralph Smalley. *Photo by David Himmel.*

In 2002, Lake of the Woods and Greenwoods Camps became part of CampGroup, a privately owned family business that owns fourteen overnight and day camps. Lake of the Woods, Greenwoods, The Glen and The Grove are the only camps located west of the Appalachian Mountains. What did this mean for Lake of the Woods and Greenwoods? Nothing. Dayna remains a shareholder, and she and her staff can operate without the watchful eye of Big Brother monitoring every move. The Hardin era, fifteen years old now, is safe from outsiders. That dome is still intact.

The Glen and The Grove

"It was my best/worst idea I ever had," Dayna said about The Glen and The Grove. "It's the best because it's so successful, but it created a lot of work for me personally."

As early as 1993, Marc was pressured to open a two-week camp. He resisted. However, he did compromise with Dayna to let the youngest campers in Iroquois and Hockaday leave a week early if they chose. By the mid-2000s, the opportunity for a full two-week camp presented itself when the farm next door went up for sale. Lake of the Woods and Greenwoods were at capacity, and Dayna knew that the market was prime since no other camp offered such a program. And so The Glen and The Grove were born. They were built from farm to finish in only a year.

The twenty-acre property through the woods along the edge of the Lake of the Woods Golf Course proved problematic as soon as the logging was completed. Because the land was so flat, nothing would drain. So the day that camp ended, hundreds of thousands of tons of filler dirt were trucked in. Three buildings were built, each one made up two cabins. A pool was built, then tennis courts, a soccer field, a basketball court, a volleyball court, an archery range and a Campcraft-like area. The old blue farmhouse was turned to a lounge and quarters for the staff. The final nail was pounded in on opening day in 2005.

"I look at it and I think, 'How did I build that in a year?'" Dayna said. "I still don't think my builder knew I was on Chicago time. He'd call me at seven o'clock in the morning, Michigan time, every day, six in Chicago. He was my wake-up call for a year."

In that year, programs were instituted, staff was hired and campers were enrolled. Through an impeccable reputation and the unstoppable promotional efforts of Dayna and her staff, the inaugural year had ninety girls at The Glen and seventy boys at The Grove, which is only a handful more than Lake of the Woods had in 1935. In fact, the speed of putting the camps together is reminiscent of how the Greenbergs put their camp together. And like the original, The Glen and The Grove grew fast. There were six cabins in 2005 and eight the next year. Another two cabins were built in 2009, and the eleventh and twelfth cabins were built in 2010.

These new two-week camps attract a wide range of campers. Eight- and four-week summer camps have historically been the preference of Jewish families. But there's a great big non-Jewish world out there that doesn't even consider four weeks as an option, so two-week sessions suit many just fine. As a result, The Glen and The Grove pull from more countries and states than the other two.

They function much like the bigger camps next door. The kids can take all of the same activities, though most are separate from Lake of the Woods and Greenwoods. The old ski annex in Campcraft that was once used for advanced skiers has been transformed into The Glen and Grove Sailing and Canoeing Docks. In between those docks and The Girls' Waterfront is The

Glen and Grove Ski Dock, with two Malibu boats to its name. Campers and counselors eat in the Mess Hall and report sickness in the Infirmary—not in that order or because of any relation. There are even Color Days at the end of each session. Their colors are pink and green for The Glen and blue and red for The Grove, though they were originally blue and orange, but with those being Chicago Bears and Fighting Illini colors, they seemed a bit overused.

Every two weeks, a new swath of campers rolls in and the camp rotates, much like movies portray 1920s speakeasies quickly flipping over to legit joints when the coppers make a raid. The Glen opens the season and The Grove closes it. While one camp is out of session, the staff is left to assist in activity areas and shack up with a boys' or girls' cabin. The Glen and Grove staffers become bunk-aunties and bunk-uncles, more commonly referred to as bunties and bunkles.

When Lake of the Woods opened, there was no such thing as a four-week session. It was stay nine or stay home. Now with a two-week camp, the biggest question remains: Is that enough time for my kid to get through homesickness? Dayna thought it was. "It's like anything else, in a four-week camp the most homesick kid is fine after two weeks because he can see the light. In a two-week camp, he's fine after the first week for the same reason."

So, the benefits of camp—no matter how long a kid stays—remain. "They still say their camp friends are their best friends," Dayna said. "It still has the ability to connect kids to other kids and make them feel like this is their place."

The reality is that camp is bigger. It's louder and brighter, and on the surface, it hardly resembles itself from fifteen years ago, and even less so from almost eighty years ago. But what, if anything, does?

Chapter 12

THE CLOSING CAMPFIRE

Home is the place where, when you have to go there, they have to take you in.
—Robert Frost

So what, so things change. They have to. If they didn't, we'd still be swimming around in the primordial ooze stuck somewhere between tadpole and ape. I'd like to see a tadpole play capture the flag, make a fire and burn a rope.

Laurie said that he never wanted a big camp, afraid it would lose its intimacy. But a new owner always meant growth. Seegerville evolved from the Greenberg era, and the Hardin era evolved from Seegerville. "There are really nice things about having a small camp," Dayna said. "But what do you do when there are four kids in Iroquois who don't like each other? Or want to play football?"

New changes allow for new ways to have fun. The new shower house has become the playing field of showball. Kevin Gerbie and Eric Umans will both be Mohawk campers in 2012. They explain it as a twisted kind of dodgeball: the object of the game is to whip a volleyball at the bar above the stalls that holds the curtains so it falls down, exposing anybody in a stall. And here's the thing: no matter how different campers are today than they were one, two, four or seven decades ago, boys will be boys. Whether it's rat-tailing or showball, playfully violent games in the nude will always be entertaining.

Some changes end up going back to the beginning, like with Campership at Lake of the Woods. Honor Camper went away to make room for Indian

Princess, which went away to make room for today's Campership, a DC idea. Funny enough, she had no idea that Campership was done almost exactly like the classic Honor Camper, but with less singing and whimsy. Will today's girls remember Campership sixty years from now like Alice, Agnes, Cookie, Lois and Roselle remember Honor Camper? Probably. Because things at camp will always be the same.

No matter how long you're gone from the place, how many trees are uprooted, Big Houses knocked down or new cabins slapped together, camp is the same. No matter where Circle takes place, how many kids roam the waterfront, paint themselves all black for Color Days or learn that their team won via skywriting, camp is the same. Cut it any way you want, camp is the same.

Some have said that once you leave camp, you can't go back. And that's wrong. You can always go back. You can always pick right back up, right where you were with your friends like you never said goodbye on that last day.

When I visited camp in 2011, I was shocked by how comfortable it felt. The kids sang and shouted and played. The counselors goofed around with one another and their campers. There was still a mad dash to Canteen after lunch. I'm telling you, change the names and faces and I could have been a camper again. Hell, keep the names and faces; I could be a counselor again.

There's a lot of talk of tradition at camp. The greatest tradition that has echoed through the years

> "When I left that first summer…That drive down 47th½ Street…I was bawling my eyes out. I thought, 'These are the best friends I'll ever have.'"
> —"Big" James Boulware
>
> "I looked at camp as a place for acceptance. It was a place of pure friendships. There were friends everywhere you turned. And they are still some of my best friends today."
> —Emily "Ferdie" Ferdman

has been the feeling of safety, or rather, the feeling that camp is home. And it's perfect. In 1999, I wrote a song with Kevin "Lofty" Loft for the Staff Show called "Stealing Home Again." It's a love song about camp. The opening line is, "Every moment is precious/Even the worst day is still a good day." It was hack sentimental hogwash, I know. But it's true.

"At forty years old, I remember all the bad stuff," Dan said. "Watching my brother get hit by a car is not a good memory. But it's become one. My memories are perfect—even the bad days like losing the lake swim and getting yelled at by my captain. But together, it was all perfect—the 'perfect summer.' In my mind's eye, my ten summers are now perfect. Even if I couldn't light the goddam fire and burn the string."

Remember, even Mrs. G. said that her happiest days were at camp. And most of them were spent after her husband died just before the seventh summer. But it's not just old bulls like us who wax optimistic about the absent bad days; thirteen-year-old Dylan Hardin often said, "Even a bad day at camp is still better than a good day at home." And this is coming from a kid whose mom is a golf cart ride away. But he can separate the two. He gets it, just like any other kid. And that's pretty damn cool.

You won't find a more forgiving and understanding and encouraging place and time than the days at Lake of the Woods and Greenwoods Camps. I knew that at the end of my first summer. So I can tell you that you can always go home to camp. You can always go home because it's always right there in your lungs and your bones and your memories. That's true. And you'll never be an orphan with these memories. And so they go on and on, ever changing, ever staying the same. And always home. Even after the last campfire has turned to smoke.

EPILOGUE

In 1990, David Cuffy was my best friend. We were eleven years old and in Chippewa cabin. Cuffy was the most popular and revered camper throughout all of camp. He even had a theme song to the tune of "Brass Monkey" by the Beastie Boys: "Dave Cuffy/That Fluffy Cuffy." I was new at camp, and he was a three-year veteran. It was good having him as a pal to show me the ropes. And like me, he was one of the few campers not from the North Shore of Chicago. I was a south suburb kid, a White Sox fan by geographical definition. Cuffy was from California. I think he rooted for the Dodgers.

Cuffy was only a four-weeker, and I was at camp for all eight weeks. I was saddened knowing that I'd have to spend the second half of my summer without my best friend. A few days before the end of the first session, Cuffy and I were wandering around camp, talking, laughing, throwing sticks… We made our way to the small fishing dock that used to be between the Sail Dock and the Boys' Waterfront and sat there as the little waves from boat wakes nipped at our feet. At one point, Cuffy laid down on his stomach so he could reach into the water for a skipping rock.

"It sucks you're leaving," I told him.

"We can still be best friends," he said.

"How?"

He looked up at me and said, "Next year, Davey." Then he skipped the living hell out of that rock.

But Cuffy didn't come back the next year. He never came back to camp again. I didn't know it until I wrote this book—that it was that moment on the dock that kept me coming back to camp year after year. It wasn't in the hopes that Cuffy would return; it was that there was always next year to get even more out of it and put more in. You know, I grew into my skin as I browned it on sailboats on Lake of the Woods, and I got used to the way it fit. I became me at camp. All my confidence, my attitude and my aptitude were found and figured out because of all of those summers and all of those people and all of those friends.

I'm grateful for my memories of Lake of the Woods and Greenwoods Camps. They make me, me. I'm even more grateful that there are still memories being made by people who will likely never know David Cuffy.

Rendering of the current properties.

BIBLIOGRAPHY

Camp 50th Reunion Home Movie, July 21, 1985. Courtesy of Ceil Rothbart, Greenberg Family Collection.

Camp Max Strauss. http://www.jbbbsla.org/jbbbsla/?page=27.

Center for Jewish History. http://www.cjh.org.

Decatur Republican. "Lake of the Woods Camp." Found in *A Scrap Book History of Early Decatur, Michigan & Vicinity: 1829–1976.* Vol. 1. Edited by Catherine Howland. N.p.: Decatur Bicentennial Committee, 1976. Originally published in 1935.

Dobuzinskis, Alex. "Eternity with Marilyn Monroe Goes Back on Auction Block." Reuters. http://blogs.reuters.com/fanfare/2009/10/15/eternity-with-marilyn-monroe-goes-back-on-auction-block.

Encyclopedia of Chicago. "Orphanges." http://encyclopedia.chicagohistory.org/pages/937.html.

Greenberg, Florence. "My Life Story." Unpublished. Courtesy of Ceil Rothbart, Greenberg Family Collection.

Greenberg, Florence P. Audio interview, Winnipeg Jewish Community Council Office, July 13, 1981. Courtesy of Ceil Rothbart, Greenberg Family Collection.

Greenwoods Camp programs. Unpublished, property of the camp.

Jewish Big Sisters. http://www.jewishbigsisters.org.

Lake of the Woods Camp programs. Unpublished, property of the camp.

Li'l Abner. "Sadie Hawkins Day." http://www.lil-abner.com/sadiehawk.html.

Manitoba Historical Society. http://mhs.mb.ca.

Resnicoff, Arnold E. "Greenberg Family." Unpublished. Courtesy of Ceil Rothbart, Greenberg Family Collection.

Schwartz, Agnes. "A Very Special Reunion." *Chicago Jewish News*, September 5–11, 2003.

ThinkExist. http://thinkexist.com.

Time. "Medicine: Polio Scare." July 26, 1948.

University of Chicago Library. "Research Resources on Chicago, Jazz, and the Great Migration." http://www.lib.uchicago.edu/e/su/cja/greatmigration.html.

Wikipedia. "Coxsackie A virus." http://en.wikipedia.org/wiki/Coxsackie_A_virus.

———. "History of poliomyelitis." http://en.wikipedia.org/wiki/History_of_poliomyelitis.

INTERVIEWS

Bates, Deb. Interviewed by author, March 10, 2012.

Bates, Douglas. Interviewed by author, August 16, 2011.

Boulware, James. Interviewed by author, August 7, 2011.

Burns, Robert. Interviewed by author, February 27, 2012.

Chatfield, Guy. Interviewed by author, February 13, 2012.

Cohn, Dana. Interviewed by author, August 16, 2011.

Cohn, Lauren. Interviewed by author, January 18, 2012.

Dorn, Shana. Interviewed by author, March 14, 2012.

Ferdman, Emily. Interviewed by author, March 15, 2012.

Frick, Sam. Interviewed by author, March 14, 2012.

Gerbie, Kevin. Interviewed by author, March 14, 2012.

Gill, Laura. Interviewed by author, February 9, 2012.

Goldberg, Michael. Interviewed by author, February 22, 2012.

Goldman, Daniel. Interviewed by author, March 2, 2012.

Goldwin, Bob. Interviewed by author, August 16, 2011.

Goldwin, Daniel. Interviewed by author, January 28, 2012.

Hardin, Dayna. Interviewed by author, July 31, 2011.

Hearth, Billy. Interviewed by author, January 22, 2012.

Hechter, Roselle. Interviewed by author, June 6, 2011.

Himmel, Tod. Interviewed by author, August 4, 2011.

Howe, Gerred. Interviewed by author, August 2, 2011.

Jacobs, Holly. Interviewed by author, February 9, 2012.

Jacobson, Stacey. Interviewed by author, March 4, 2012.

Jernagin, Mary. Interviewed by author, August 6, 2011.

Katz, Lois. Interviewed by author, June 25, 2011.

Kessler, Ryan. Interviewed by author, March 6, 2012.

Lebovitz, Amy. Interviewed by author, February 8, 2012.

Lebovitz, Zach. Interviewed by author, February 27, 2012.

Migoya, José Miguel. Interviewed by author, February 12, 2012.

Migoya, Pablo Dragon. Interviewed by author, August 25, 2011.

Miner, Jeffrey T. Interviewed by author, January 11, 2012.

Nicholson, Anthony. Interviewed by author, January 3, 2012.

Parker, Melissa. Interviewed by author, March 4, 2012.

Poncher, Cookie. Interviewed by author, June 6, 2011.

Rosenberg, Linda. Interviewed by author, December 12, 2011.

Rothbart, Ceil. Interviewed by author, July 24, 2011; August 1, 2011.

Saewitz, Lindsay. Interviewed by author, January 2, 2012.

Schindel, Alice. Interviewed by author, June 6, 2011.

Schwartz, Agnes. Interviewed by author, June 6, 2011.

Seeger, Laurie. Interviewed by author, June 20, 2011.

Seeger, Marc. Interviewed by author, May 23, 2011.

Solow, Sheldon. Interviewed by author, March 2, 2012.

Troy, Joshua. Interviewed by author, January 18, 2012.

Umans, Eric. Interviewed by author, July 30, 2011.

Werner, Amy. Interviewed by author, March 4, 2012.

Windomaker, John. Interviewed by author, August 12, 2011.

Yanow, Lauren. Interviewed by author, January 11, 2012.

Zacher, Rory. Interviewed by author, December 7, 2012.

ABOUT THE AUTHOR

David Himmel is an author, essayist, playwright and editor. A former radio personality in Las Vegas, he currently serves as the principal of the creative firm Himmel, Ink., as well as the managing editor of *Chicago Health* magazine. David has received awards for his stage and film productions, and his work is featured in national and regional magazines. He spent ten summers at Greenwoods Camp as a camper and counselor. He remains an avid sailor. David lives in Chicago. Visit his website at himmelink.com.

Visit us at
www.historypress.net